George Frederick Cameron

Lyrics on Freedom, Love and Death

George Frederick Cameron

Lyrics on Freedom, Love and Death

ISBN/EAN: 9783744774307

Printed in Europe, USA, Canada, Australia, Japan

Cover: Foto ©Thomas Meinert / pixelio.de

More available books at **www.hansebooks.com**

Yea, Fame, or bread, or whatever thou be —
I shed the wine of my life for thee !

LYRICS

— ON —

FREEDOM, LOVE AND DEATH

BY THE LATE

GEORGE FREDERICK CAMERON

EDITED BY HIS BROTHER

CHARLES J. CAMERON, M.A.

QUEEN'S UNIVERSITY, KINGSTON

———

KINGSTON
LEWIS W. SHANNON, 67 PRINCESS ST.
BOSTON
ALEXANDER MOORE, 3 SCHOOL ST.
1887

PRINTED AT THE DAILY NEWS OFFICE, KINGSTON.

Contents.

Contents.

Contents.

Contents.

Contents.

Contents.

Contents.

Contents.

Preface.

TO THE CRITIC.

In accordance with the last wishes of the author, the first portion of his manuscript is here submitted to your judgment. This volume represents about one fourth of his life work. If it is well received, the rest will follow in due course. This is a Canadian contribution to our common literature, and I hope that it may be thought by the old world a worthy interpreter of our younger and broader national life.

Of the Lyrics on Freedom, those on Cuba were written between the ages of fourteen and nineteen, on France about his eighteenth or nineteenth year, and on Russia between then and the time of his death. The verses prefixed to each are from an address written by the author while a student of Queen's University, and inserted as an introduction to that which follows.

In its issue of Friday, Sept. 18th, 1885, the *Montreal Witness* contained, as its first item of Canadian News, the following :—

Preface.

On Thursday night, George F. Cameron, late editor of the *Kingston News*, died suddenly. He was a graceful writer and a prominent Canadian poet.

This was the sum of the story of his life, so far as the world could tell it. The high position which he took in Canadian literature he won almost in a day, on a few lyrics published in his own paper and in the columns of the Queen's College Journal. The preface to this conclusion you will find here.

Young, as the world counts time, at thirty years of age he had run the whole *gamut* of its pleasures and its pains. There was to him a terrible sameness about it all.—

> Golden prospects and ominous clouds :
>> Impassable walks and level drives :
> Glittering silks and colorless shrouds :
>> Flattering records and shattered lives,

These were the elements of its every change, and to his eternal *quid novi ?* it had nothing further to answer. So that he who had begun life by being an enthusiast had almost finished it by becoming a cynic.

> All heartsick and headsick and weary,
>> Sore wounded, oft struck in the strife,
> I ask is there end of this dreary
>> Dark pilgrimage called by us life ?

Preface.

I ask, is there end of it—any ?
  If any, when comes it anigh ?
I would die, not the one death, but many
  To know and be sure I should die.

To know that Somewhere—in the distance,
  When Nature shall take back my breath,
I shall add up the sum of existence
  And find that its total is—death !

It was impossible, being what he was, that his poetry should be free from occasional pessimism. This was the natural product of the circumstances of his life. It was necessary from the character of the age in which he wrote : it was inevitable from the quality of his own mind.

It is not without meaning that he sings in the last Springtime of his life,

We reach for rest, and the world wheels by us
  And leaves us each in our vale of tears :
Till the green sod covers and nought comes nigh us
  With hopes and fears.

Nor that in its last month we hear him say, as he looks out into the unknown.

For we shall rest. The brain that planned.
  That thought or wrought or well or ill,

Preface.

At gaze like Joshua's moon shall stand,
    Not working any work or will :
While eye, and lip, and heart, and hand
    Shall all be still—shall all be still !

The truest life of a poet is written in his songs. Why, then, go further ? *If they hear not Moses and the prophets,*—You know the rest.

From the Present he asked nothing : and from the Future—but, let him speak for himself :—

We only ask it as our share
    That, when your day-star rises clear,
A perfect splendor in the air,
    A glory ever far and near,
Ye write such words as these—of those who were !

I have one favor to ask of the critic, and one only. Read him, before you review him.

Remember that he is with the dead, and do him justice. I ask no more, and the editor of these songs needs to ask no more.

How will the world receive him ? With coldness, may be : it may be with pleasure. In any case it will matter little to him, who, as I pen these words, sleeps peacefully beneath the daisies in the land which gave him birth.

128 Union St., Kingston,
    October 6th, 1887.

HIS LIFE.

GEORGE FREDERICK CAMERON, the author of the following poems, the eldest son of James Grant Cameron, and Jessie Sutherland, was born in New Glasgow, Nova Scotia, September 24th, 1854. He received his preliminary education at the High School of his native town, and had read the greater part of Virgil and Cicero in the original before his fourteenth year. Even at this age he employed the most of his spare time in poetry. Removing with his family to Boston in the spring of 1869, he entered the Boston University of Law, in 1872. After graduation, he entered the law office of Dean, Butler and Abbot in the same city. From this period until 1882 his attention was mainly devoted to literature and he was a frequent contributor to the *Commercial Bulletin*, *Traveller*, *Courier* and *Transcript* of the new Athens of America. In 1882 he entered Queen's University and was the prize poet in 1883.

In March of the same year he became Editor of the Kingston *News*, which position he held until a few weeks before his death. The latter event took place during a visit to the country, where, on the 17th of September, he expired of heart disease after a few hours sickness.

For the last two years of his life he had been greatly troubled with insomnia, getting not more than from two to three hours sleep per night.

He married Ella, the eldest daughter of Billings Amey, Esq., of Millhaven, on the twenty-second of August, 1883. His wife and an infant daughter survive him.

That the author did not bubble over in his verse with loyalty to the throne and all it represents was perhaps his infirmity. I tried to persuade him of the advantages such a course would offer to a poor poet like himself, but, I regret to say, to no purpose. Whether the reason of failure lay in the weakness of the cause or in his want of faith in my sincerity is a moot question with me to this day.

Dedication.

TO

JESSIE SUTHERLAND CAMERON.

Oh, can there be in any word or line
  For mother-love a fitting recompense ?—
  For mother-love immortal, or intense
As if it were immortal and divine,
  And more perceptible to the bodily sense ?

If recompense there be in word or phrase
  For such a love forever brimming o'er,
  Despising common tide-mark, common shore,
Watering the flowers about life's desert ways
  And causing them to flourish more and more :

If recompense there be in poem or prose,
  I, who desire to know it, know it not :
  It lies beyond me still, though I have sought—
That I might pay thine own to thee—to close
  My hand upon it in the maze of thought.

Yet, if I may not pay my debt complete,
  Still, as a slight percentage from me, take
  My love and this : a later wave may break
In richer ripples, mother, at thy feet :
  But,—take these now, and keep them for my sake !

Lyrics on Freedom.

There have been kings ! There have been kings !—
Proclaim it while it is to-day :
For lo ! the ages pass away,—
And men will doubt there were such things
Ere many centuries decay.

3

Cuba.

Long time she labored sore, and lay
   The sport of Spain's imperial whim,
While cowards, in a coward's pay,
   Tore shrieking Freedom limb from limb.

But lo! A better morrow broke
   To light her every vale and hill,—
For, though she wears the Spanish yoke,
   And speaks her Master's language still;

And though she takes her laws as yet
   From o'er the sea—what Spain hath lost
Spain will not, in an hour, forget,
   Nor what the losing lesson cost.

O Cuba! May the Eternal ring
   Thee round about, and make thee free,—
A flawless gem, a perfect thing,
   The sunniest Island of the sea.

January 1st, 1884.

Proem.

No Spanish blood I boast, but to
   That holy hope of man I cling
   Which makes him free of lord and king;
Who asks of me a reason due
   I give it to him while I sing:

For I am of that forlorn hope
   That is the only hope of man,—
From corner stone to curve and cope
   I am a cosmopolitan!

1868—1873.

In 1869 the Island was one scene of carnage. Frightful atrocities were committed by the Spanish troops in Havana and other cities. Up to August 1872, 13,000 Cubans had been killed in battle, and 43,500 prisoners put to death. Over 150,000 soldiers had been sent out from Spain.—C. J. C.

SHE IS NOT MINE.

She is not mine—this land of tears,
  But her high cause is mine, and was,
  And shall be, till my thought shall pause
Upon the measure of its years
  To ponder over larger laws.

And since her cause is mine, and man's—
  Else it were never mine—I hold
  That I may speak in accents bold
For Liberty and all her plans,
  And her high phases manifold.

I would not speak for blood, nor will
  I dream too long of that long lease
  Of days when war and strife shall cease,—
When that accursed cry of "*kill*"!
  Shall change into the calm of peace:

She is not Mine.

.

But yet—I speak my thought—but yet,
  Should it be so that some must die
  A sacrifice for liberty,
Let tyrant blood alone be let,—
  Let despots' veins alone be dry!

Without fair Liberty to make
  The key-stone of the world's whole plan,
The arch we heap o'erhead will break,
And some fair morrow man will wake
  To find beneath the ruins—man!

MY POLITICAL FAITH.

I am not of those fierce, wild wills,
　Albeit from loins of warlike line,
　To wreck laws human and divine
Alike, that on a million ills
　I might erect one sacred shrine

To Freedom: nor again am I
　Of *these* who could be sold and bought
　To fall before a Juggernaut:
I hold all " royal right " a lie—
　Save that a royal soul hath wrought !

It is in the extreme begins
　And ends all danger: if the Few
　Would feel, or if the Many knew
This fact, the mass of fewer sins
　Would shrive them in their passing through:

O'er all God's footstool not a slave
　Should under his great glory stand,
　For men would rise, swift sword in hand,
And give each tyrant to his grave
　And freedom to each lovely land.

9

JUSTICE ?*

Again defeated, gallant land!
  Again thy hopes are in the dust:
  Again thy throat receives the thrust
From tyrant steel in tyrant hand,
  And coward lips that call it—" just."

This Justice! Perish justice—all
  And every high and noble deed,
  And every righteous cause and creed,
If it be just for men to fall
  To serve or sate a despot's greed!

This Justice! By the God who rules
  Above the spheres of thought and things,
  There is a day that comes and brings
Pure justice to the fools and tools
  Who crouch to, write or fight for kings!

*Suggested by a paragraph from the pen of some scribbler who is, and deserves
to be—nameless.- G. F. C.

FORWARD!

Soldiers, forward for your honor!
  Forward every gallant band,—
  Forward for your mother-land:
Freedom yet shall smile upon her:
  Forward, Cubans, heart and hand!

Do not tyrants, long prevailing,
  Sweep your isle with desolation?
  Drink the life-blood of your nation?
Smile to hear your widows' wailing?
  Use the sword!—'tis your salvation.

Use the sword!—with it contending
  Ye will conquer soon or late:
  Ye will make your country's fate:
Ye will see her star ascending
  Calm and beautiful and great!

BUT WORDS?

What can I give? but words—no more?
  Not now—to-day: yet words being wed
  With Truth that quickens even the dead
Have shaken thrones and Things before,—
  Have moulded men who moulded lead,

And shot it through a thousand shields
  Of despots to their thousand hearts,
  Despite their cells and felon-carts,
Their guillotines, and battle fields,—
  Yea, spite of war and all her arts!

And words may do what words have done,
  Ay, words as weak as mine are weak:
  Though, should but now the elder speak,
I need not, for to-morrow's sun
  Might seek a slave,—and vainly seek!

DEFEATED OFT.

Defeated oft,—defeated still!
   All holy is the patriot's cause :
   All holy is the sword he draws :
All holy Nature's Sinai-hill
   From which alone he takes his laws.

Weep not for those who died to-day—
   The brave who take their latest rest !
   They slumber on their mother's breast :
Their glory, mortal yesterday,
   To-day immortal stands confest.

Not even their blood is shed in vain ;—
   In fertile soil still falls such seed ;
   And from each drop that heroes bleed
A thousand heroes spring again,—
   Each drop a Cadmus-tooth, indeed.

COLUMBIA vs. FREEDOM.*

Go, vaunt Columbia's glory, ye
   Who cower beneath the glance of Spain!
   Admit that Freedom's war is vain:
Admit 'tis vulgar to be free,
   And better far to hug a chain!

Unworthy sons of worthy sires
   Go to your senate-halls, and tell
   The world that tyranny is well,
Albeit it quench fair Freedom's fires
   And make the earth a very hell!

---

*To their dishonor be it said, many of the American newspapers wrote as American statesmen (sic!) spoke against the Cubans in their magnificent struggle for Liberty. Talis liberorum virtus!

Then gaze where Caribbean waves
  Loll calm on desecrated sands ;
  Where Freedom cheers her weary bands :
Where heroes dig heroic graves
  With their own hero-hands.

Then turn again, and, if you dare,
  Pronounce that Spain is in the right :
  Pronounce his fight a holy fight :
Pronounce the Cuban cause a snare :
  Tell earth there is no right but might !

NAY, STRIKE AGAIN.

O verdured Islands of the main—
  Fair emerald glories of the sea!
Strike hard! strike fast! Nay, strike again!
  And strike—till ye are free!

Dispute each pebble and each sod,
  Each lofty mountain, mossy glen,
Fit for the footsteps of a god,
  And fit for free and noble *men!*

Shrink not from toil! the boon you crave
  Is only worthy of the brave:—
It may be worth alike a grave!

Swear to be free, or die!
  'Tis all ye need:
Cowards live on and sigh,—
  But brave men bleed!

THE CUBAN DEAD.

Oh, weep not for them, for all time shall deplore them !
  To the keeping of ages each sorrow resign :
The bard shall bewail them, a world shall weep o'er
    them,—
  Posterity make of their tombstone a shrine.

Plant not o'er their resting place ivy or willow !—
  Their deeds are immortal, tho' names be unknown ;
The soil they have freed is their winding sheet, pillow,—
  Their sepulchre, monument, glory and throne !

'TIS DONE!

'Tis done! The sword that flashed in air
  At Freedom's bidding, shattered lies :
  The wing that brushed so late the skies
Is palsied all, and in despair
  The eagle falls and darkly dies.

'Tis done! The stubborn head is bent,
  And paralyzed the rebel heart :
  And might hath been the magic art
That hath accomplished the event
  And winged the subtly poisoned dart.

'Tis done! The fratricidal strife
  Hath given to Cuba naught of gain,
  She bends submissive knee to Spain :
This battle to the very knife
  Is but a battle fought in vain.

'Tis done! The Spaniard stands at length,
  The victor's laurel on his brow:
  The heart which scorned so long to bow
Is bowed at length by tyrant strength,
  Is bowed,—and all is over now.

'Tis done! The spirit that inspired
  My earlier visions all is fled:
  The dreams on which my fancy fed
Dead as the beacon Freedom fired,
  Aye, dead—and with your hero-dead!

TAKE HEART!

Take heart! They never vainly wait
   Who wait to see redress of wrong :
   An age, though seemingly so long,
Is nought in time ; and soon or late
   Your land shall take her place among

The nations of the earth : for Right
   And Honor yet shall set her free :
   Her air, though tainted now, shall be
As pure as yonder holy light
   That smiles upon your southern sea !

Take heart! A happier day awaits
   Your weary, battling, bleeding isle,—
   A happier day, when Peace shall smile
On all that is within your gates,
   And war shall rest himself a while.

For noble deeds must bear this fruit :
   And holy Freedom yet shall stand
   Within each despot-ridden land,
The chain of slavery 'neath her foot—
   The star of Promise in her hand !

AVE ATQUE VALE!

When war is over, and thy glorious brow
   Gleams with the star of Peace and Victory;
When all thy sons at Freedom's shrine shall bow;
   When all thy daughters, fairest as they be,
   Shall learn to lisp the name of Liberty
And offer incense at her altar; *then*,
   Then in thy pride of place remember me—
The nameless bard who sung thy praises when
None other dared to sing among the sons of men!

Russia.

There Russia lightless land of pain,
    Rude region of forbidden thought,
Where Freedom, walking, clanks a chain,
    Or pines in prison till she rot :—

Where every moment breaks a heart,
    Where hope can hardly draw a breath,
Where rumbles still the hangman's cart,
    And all the air is thick with death :

Yea, Russia—sick and sad of soul,
    And, like the camel, forced to kneel,
Feels on her back the burden roll,
    And lifts again the old appeal ;

And vainly lifts it : while the throng
    Of maid, and woman, man and child,
Goes outward—singing sadder song
    Than Babel's—to Siberia's wild.

But even for *thee* there is a hope,—
  That better Ruler shall be thine,
Whose sway shall show that cell, and rope,
  Are not the seals of " Right Divine."

This failing thee—a Power shall wake
  As stern as steel, as strong as stone ;
A Power that never fails to shake
  A *too-dark* Despot from his throne :—

Rebellion's self, with vengeful hand,
  Disdaining civic wreath and robe,
Shall take the sword, and blazing brand,
  And sweep the Gorgon from the globe.

23

ALEXIS ROMANOFF.*

There are thunders of cheers on the street,
 They are smiting and striking the air:
Is it right? Is it well? Is it meet?
 What deed hath he done who is there,
That the people should lie at his feet?

What deed hath he done that we know?
 What of good unto others or us?
And what is the debt that ye owe
 Him, to fawn on and flatter him thus?—
That ye cringe to, and bow to him so?

Hath he shown a contempt of the wrong?
 Hath he shown a desire of the right?
Hath he broken the strength of the strong,
 Or supported the weak with his might,
That to meet him and greet him ye throng?

Ye freemen, whose ancestors crost
 Over anarchy's perilous sea!
How much hath your liberties cost
 That ye sell them so cheaply? that ye
Would so lightly behold them all lost?

*On the reception of the Grand Duke in Boston.

Alexis Romanoff.

Why stoop ye, if more than the name
  Of freemen remains to you now?—
Why stoop ye so swiftly to shame?
  Why darken the spark on your brow
That should leap into luminous flame?

Being freeest of those who are free,
  Being bravest of those who are brave,
Why bend you so ready a knee?
  Is Freedom the chattel and slave
Of the autocrat over the sea?

Oh, it is but a courtesy shown
  To a king, or the son of a king!
How courteous at length ye have grown!
  But courtesy—what!—must it bring
Ye to fall at the foot of a throne?

Ye had fathers both courteous and brave
  Who could die, but consent not to shame:
Ye had fathers—they sleep in the grave,
  The children of freedom and fame:—
Know ye not what they thought of a slave?—

Alexis Romanoff.

Of a slave who had chosen to lie
  In the dust when he well might be free?—
Of a slave who, when princes went by,
  Would fall with a pliable knee?
Seek their graves—and their dust will reply!

Is it dead, then—this spirit that spoke
  In the battle, the storm, and the strife?
Is it dead? Is its sceptre now broke?
  Is it dead—that it leaps not to life
On the soil where to life it first woke?

Is it dead? Do the lip and the brow
  Only worship a name at a shrine
Polluted and desecrate now—
  No longer revered as divine—
Where the noblest of ages did bow?

Oh, be men! I beseech you, be men!
  Upon you are the eyes of the earth:
Yonder History holdeth her pen
  To rate you at what you are worth,—
Disgrace not fair Freedom again!

THE "DIVINE RIGHT."

When nations from their slavery wake,
  And every band that bound them break,
Then comes the stern decree of kings—
  Subdue them, or destroy!
High through the quivering air it rings,
While Death and Famine wave their wings,
  And glut their savage joy.

The Czar, with his Damascene brand,
  Pricks the bear of the north till uncurled:
O'er the cities and towns of a perishing land
  His ominous flag is unfurled;
While the glove that late sat on the Autocrat's hand
  Is flung in the face of the world!

The " Divine Right."

Blow, winds of heaven! in all the broad land :
   Blow, winds of God! in all the broad sea :
Blow, till the sceptre is wrung from the hand
   Of the tyrant, and earth is free,
   The proud, firm song of equality !
Breathe it into each mortal ear,—
   Force it into each human soul,—
That man was born for a holier sphere
   Than a despot's base control !

Be thou an emperor, sultan, or czar,
   Priest or patriarch, queen or king,
Thou hast no right to the judgment car--
   Man is the noblest created thing !—
From the same origin—all, the same pair :
Blow on the wandering winds afar—
   Scatter it here, and scatter it there :—
Man is man's peer, only man is his peer,
   And each has a right each is bound to revere,-

The right to be free—to be true :
   The right to be true—to be free :
So whatever, my lord, is a right for you,
   The same is a right for me !

What! not a right to break
    What you have a right to bind?
What! not a right to take
    Redress for the wrongs of mankind?
What! not a right to shake
    With the catapult of the mind
The ramparts which you have built
    To shelter the throne you hold?—
To pass through the breach to your citadel—Guilt,
    And to trample your image of gold?
Oh, you would sheathe your sword to the hilt
    In the heart that would be so bold!

So, breezes! whisper the Czar
    Who tramples a beggarly land,
That perhaps, 'neath the sheen of the star
    That lights his marauding band
On their pathway of ruin and war,
    The David even now may stand
Waiting and watching—nor distant far—
    With the sling in his boyish hand,
Till a David's God shall arise in wrath
    And smite to the dust this giant of Gath.

COLUMBIA—RUSSIA!

Columbia—Russia! God above!
  Who dares to link the fame
Acquired by Freedom, Union, Love,
  With Alexander's name?
  Who dares to say Columbia's hand
Would aid the Russian smite the land
  From which our fathers came?—
If such should be, all time would brand
With contumely her banner, and
  Her virgin brow with shame!

Alliance with the northern Tsar?—
  To bid the blood of Nations flow,
To set the earth aflame with war,—
To spread it near, to fling it far,—
  To make the world a waste of woe
To drag or fall before his car?
  No!—One for many answers—No!

On hearing of a proposed alliance between Russia and the United States.

For Freedom's cause, for Freedom's cause
   The freeman's banner only flies :
For that alone his sword he draws,
   For that alone he dies.
Go, autocrat ! The hireling slave
   May dig himself a hireling's grave :—
'Twould ill become the free and brave !

WHAT MEANS THIS PAGEANTRY?*

What means this pageantry and glare ?—
  The stately tread of horses feet ?
The numerous gazers on the street,—
  This solemn roll of muffled drums,—
These banners flaunting in the air,—
These weeds the myriad mourners wear,—
  This voice of melancholy prayer ?
Pronounce !—Is it some hero comes ?

Some soldier who, in battle-plain,
  As he his country's banner bore,
Where fiercest flew the leaden rain
  Fell—fell to rise again no more :
Died, pride still vanquishing his pain,
  Died for his land,—nor died in vain ?

*On memorial services to Czar Alexander in Boston.

What means this Pageantry?

No? Then some sage to whom 'twas given
   The rugged steeps of Fame to climb ;
And high among the stars of heaven
   To write, with daring hand sublime,
   His deeds for all recurring time :—
A man of pure and humble birth
   Born heir to deeds of high emprize,
Who to the chariot wheels of earth
   Chained some new spirit of the skies,
Like that triumphant Franklin gave
To be man's mighty, humble slave ?

Some meteoric son of song
   Who climbed Parnassus' lofty height,
And from the summit poured along
   A strain of majesty and might ?
Who from the dewy wings of Night
   Shook out the latent stars of fire
And, wrapped within this cloud of light,
   Swept with trained hand the sounding lyre
Till nations all did prostrate fall
   And hail him prophet, bard, and sire ?

What means this Pageantry?

No, none of these.—The day is past
  When son of song or sage could claim
More than all men may have at last,—
  A grave—and a forgotten name!
For czars and emperors and kings,—
  For those who most their fellows wrong,—
The temple's sacred organ rings,
The poet from his closet brings
  The tribute of a servile song!

OUR POETS.

These men to loose or burst the galling chains
   Of those who mourn in darkness over sea!
These men—who feel a fever in their veins
   At every moon change—these to set men free!

These—these!—who sing in rapture of the Czar
   And howl their hallelujahs in his ears
To bruise the head of that grim monster—war,
   To close the eye of bitterness and tears!

These men of servile souls and servile songs
   To name the day when despotism shall cease!
These men, forsooth, to right the people's wrongs
   And give the world her harvest-time of Peace!

What can he know of joys or miseries—
   Yon vain, luxurious fool, who lolls at ease
And sips the foam alone upon the cup?

Whoe'er would know or one or all of these
   Must take the ponderous chalice, hold it up—
And drink life's vintage to its very lees!

THE CZAR.

They say I hate the Czar.   I hate
  All wrong in any high or low;
In men of small or large estate,
  In any friend or any foe:

And something of the Czar I hate,
  And, holding him as only clay,
Unlike a craven coward, straight
  Back to his royal self I say :—

Thy reign was bitter, barren, blind, and bad :
  Thy life was black, and blackened other ones
That else had known no sorrow, or had had
  Some of God's light within them and His Son's,—
Within them and about : but o'er thy day
The curtain closes, and they see thee—clay !

This to his teeth.   And then to those
  Paid by him—nothing : they are naught.
Truth goes wherever manhood goes,
  And fears not either shell or shot :
And God hath put the liar's lot
  Beyond the chance of day or date,—
And if the Czar can, or cannot,.
  Why, He who made them all can wait !

TO THE CZAR.

If ever fell the wrath of God
   Upon a bitter fool, and blind,
Who stained with blood a ready rod   •
   And sought and slew his fellow-kind,
   And banished mercy from his mind,
And with a level face severe, --
   In which no trace did any find
Of any hope for any year,—

Walked on and over all that came
   Betwixt him and his tyrant will,
And knew not any shade of shame,
   And only heard and heeded still
   That fierce old Roman cry of "*kill!*"-
Then, Autocrat, and all unjust!
   'Twill light on thee and burn, until
That heart of thine shall beat to dust.

To the Czar.

Yea, Czar of every Russia crowned!
  The meanest hind that follows plough,
Or whistles to his yellow hound,
  Is more a monarch than art thou!
  He wears a hope upon his brow,
And he dare lift his eyes above :—
  But, sightless despot, answer now—
Where moves the thing that thou dost love?

Or, where is that of man or beast
  That gives thee kindly thought or care?
From North to South, from West to East,
  Say, rises for thee anywhere
  From honest heart an honest prayer?
No! Though your messenger should run
  And scan the spaces of the air
He would not light on any one.

To the Czar.

O fool! and greater—filling throne!—
  Why is a price within thine hand
For wisdom? still thy people groan,
  And still they groan at thy command.
Can'st thou not learn nor understand
That Freedom will not suffer thrall?
  That he who fain would rule a land
Must rule by love—or not at all?

No? Then from out the pregnant womb
  Of time-to-be shall come a day
As dire to thee as that of Doom,
  And it shall draw a sword and slay:
  And it shall speak to thee and say,—
As darkly onward thou dost grope,—
  See written o'er thine every way—
" *Who enters here, abandon hope!* "

THE CZAR.

What is there in thy greatness that is great,—
    Thou, loveless as that other, loved by none?
Or, where moves man that envies thee thy fate,—
    All-evil worker, and all evil one?

Still to be hated with a whole heart's hate,
    Known and remembered but for ill deeds done,
This is forever, Tyrant! thine estate
    Beneath the crimson circle of the sun!

Watch well, O world! Right is not always wrong:
The ghosts of his own works about him throng.

Watch well—nor envy him his hour of calm,
    Ere they arise and put forth strength, and strip
The blood-stained purple from the royal sham,
    And curse the white-lipped leper to his lip!

Feb. 16, 1884.

France.

Next she, whose eddying humor went
　Through both the scales of change and chance,
At length, for once at least, content,
　Demands a line—the land of France.

A host of Sovereigns have been hers
　Since first commenced our humbler rule,
And some were bad, and some were worse,
　One was a tyrant, one a fool.

And one, or two, I need not name,—
　I know you have them in your mind,—
For they have found their proper fame,—
　Were tyrant both and fool combined.

France.

And she has wearied of them each,
  And parted with them, one by one,
And told them in divinest speech
  And firmest, that their day was done.

And beckoning Freedom to her side,—
  A calm-pulsed Freedom,—not again
That froward, fiendish fool who dyed
  Of old, with crimson hue, the Seine:—

And walking with her up the slope
  Of peaceful, civic life at last,
She sees the perfect higher hope,
  And turns her back upon the Past.

And none would wish thee worse than this:
  That still thy glory may advance;
And that no good that *is* may miss
  Thy shore, O lovely land of France!

THY SKY IS DIM.

Thy sky is dim but yet I see,
   Methinks, anear thy shore
The star that shines above the free
   Arise to set no more :
And from that star a light doth spring
A light of heaven's own wakening.

But swear it, Frenchmen, by the days
   Of anguish ye have known,
That never more shall despot raise
   In France the despot's throne !
Your hands are laid to Freedom's plough,--
Oh, look not back, nor falter now !

The memory of what hath been—
   Be that your warning light
To keep the civil scabbard clean,
   The civil sabre bright :
And bear in mind, no mutual good
Can come from fostering mutual feud !

Thy Sky is Dim.

Ye need not fear the invader's arm,
　His strength is but a boast :
But fear what most can work you harm,
　Ay, fear yourselves the most !
The flesh wound may, 'tis true, annoy :
The inward canker will destroy.

Let faction, then, this moment cease,
　Or but exist to be
Exerted in the cause of peace
　And heaven-born liberty,
Of all that makes a nation's name
Beam brighter on the scroll of Fame !

So, Frenchmen, shall the glories old
　That to your land belong,
With glories to be hers, be told
　In golden speech and song :
So shall the children on her breast
And all her lovers call her blest.

THE FUTURE?

Oh, what shall the future unravel,
   The future for which thou hast bled,
For which thou hast suffered in travail,—
   Of lustre or cloud for thy head?
Wilt thou love Peace as in the beginning?
As thou did'st, ere the day of thy sinning?
   As thou did'st, ere the perilous strife,
That a tyrant thought well worth his winning,
   Left thee lonely with only thy life?

Oh, shall it be sadness or laughter—
   Oh, shall it be gladness or tears
Shall come to thee, Beautiful, after
   The lapse of the fluctuant years?—
After the flight of the flying—
After the death of the dying—
   The swift-flying, swift-dying days?
Say, shall it be singing or sighing?
   Say, shall it be censure, or praise

The Future?

Of the day of thy deadliest error
 The day of the blood and the brand;
Of the day of thy darkness and terror
 Rude shocking and shaking the land?
Oh, what shall the writers, the sages,
The learned compilers of pages
 Say unto thee? What shall it be?
From out the deep mouth of the ages
 Oh, what shall there come unto thee?

Is it broken, thy faith, or but shaken?
 Is it dead, or only asleep?
Shall it waken again, shall it waken
 A light on a desolate deep?—
A light like the burst of the morning,
To warn thee with terrible warning
 Away from the breakers that roar,
With a voice that should silence thy scorning,
 On the iron-bound tempest-scarred shore?

The Future ?

Shall the black-foaming chalice of sorrow
  Be held to thy star-litten lips ?
Shall the sun that should light thee to-morrow
  Be blind with a total eclipse ?
Shall it be of thine own bitter potion
To see it sink down in the ocean
  All spiritless, cheerless, and cold,--
Deprived of the luminous motion
  That gladdened its being of old ?

Shall the peoples in jubilant chorus
  Fling anthems of praise in thine ears,
Or shall clamors and curses sonorous
  Upward float from the throat of the years ?
Shall thy portion be banning or blessing,
Shall thy portion be scorn or caressing,
  If any in Liberty's fight
Should falter in future, expressing
  That thou art the cause of their flight ?

The Future ?

Then thunders of curses assailing
   Shall fall on thy desolate head ;
While earth to her centre is wailing
   The innocent blood thou hast shed :
The faithful who followed shall shun thee,
The darkness of hell be upon thee—
   Stern retribute justice but meet ;—
And the laurels that chivalry won thee
   Fall faded and dead at thy feet.

But, if they who are writing thy story
   Bid those who seek freedom take heed
That the gore on thy hands is not glory,
   Nor glory each desperate deed :
Should Freedom uprising, forgetting
The sharp fratricidal blood-letting,
   To those who are seeking her tell
That this mighty upheaving, upsetting
   Was all for the best, it is well.

The Future ?

Then out of the sea of thy slaughters
　　The sun of pure wisdom shall rise ;
Earth's sons, and her beautiful daughters,
　　Shall echo thy praise to the skies,
And thank thee, O France, in their gladness,
For showing the madness of madness
　　In characters written in flame,
And place with the cypress of sadness
　　Upon thee the laurel of Fame !

IN AFTER DAYS.

I will accomplish that and this,
    And make myself a thorn to Things—
    Lords, councillors and tyrant kings—
Who sit upon their thrones and kiss

The rod of Fortune; and are crowned
    The sovereign masters of the earth
    To scatter blight and death and dearth
Wherever mortal man is found.

I will do this and that, and break
    The backbone of their large conceit,
    And loose the sandals from their feet,
And show 'tis holy ground they shake.

So sang I in my earlier days,
    Ere I had learned to look abroad
    And see that more than monarchs trod
Upon the form I fain would raise.

In After Days.

Ere I, in looking toward the land
   That broke a triple diadem,
   That grasped at Freedom's garment hem,
Had seen her, sword and torch in hand,

A freedom-fool: ere I had grown
   To know that Love is freedom's strength—
   France taught the world that truth at length!—
And Peace her chief foundation stone.

Since then, I temper so my song
   That it may never speak for blood;
   May never say that ill is good;
Or say that right may spring from wrong:

Yet am what I have ever been—
   A friend of Freedom, staunch and true,
   Who hate a tyrant, be he—you—
A people,—sultan, czar, or queen!

In After Days.

And then the Freedom-haters came
  And questioned of my former song,
  If *now* I held it right, or wrong :
And still my answer was the same :—

The good still moveth towards the good :
  The ill still moveth towards the ill :
  But who affirmeth that we will
Not form a nobler brotherhood

When ~~rabid~~ *communists,* fanatics, ~~and~~ those
  Who howl their " *vives* " to Freedom's name
  And yet betray her unto shame,
Are dead and coffined with her foes.

Columbia.

And last, Columbia, at her feet
   The ruins of three giant wars,
Comes, robed in laurel, all complete,
   Her forehead garlanded with stars !

COLUMBIA.

The first, and most sublime
   Of all the lands
That ask reward of Time,
   Columbia stands.

For hope divinely fair
   Look not to Rome
And Athens!—Look not there;
   But here—at home.

For blood that she hath spilt,
   Let after days disclose
Where blame shall be : the guilt
   Be on her foes !

OUR HERO DEAD.*

Come, sons of Massachusetts! come
With stately step, with beat of drum,
  In proud and long array:
Nor mourn ye now the brave, nor weep
O'er those who sleep the soldier's sleep,—
  Who are not here to-day. .
Aye, come ye here for whom they bled—
The turf lie lightly on their head!—
  And come with high and reverent tread,
The tribute which ye owe the dead,
  Our hero-dead, to pay.

Our hero-dead!   When rude alarms
Awoke a slumbering land to arms;
  When Freedom's hope a moment failed;
When Freedom's star a moment paled;
  When traitors sought to flee or fled;
When red Rebellion's hand assailed
  The truths for which their fathers bled;
Who seized the flag they loved, and nailed
  It to the mast?   Our hero-dead!

*On the unveiling of the monument on Boston common to the Soldiers who fell
in the war of the Rebellion.

55

Our Hero Dead.

They came from cottage and from hall
As to some lordly festival,
   And yet with sterner look, perchance,
    For deep resolve was in each glance,
To answer Union's trumpet-call.
On every hill, in every vale
   The sabre clashed, the anvil rang ;
And on these came to breast the gale
   Of war, and prove from whom they sprang :—
From every vale, from every hill
These heroes came, and with a will,—
   For still the Syren Freedom sang.

What though on many a crumbling stone
Is stamped that mournful word—" Unknown " ?
   What though some sleep in alien soil,—
    For battle claimed her share of spoil,—
   We reap the harvest of their toil :
The wildest storms of war they braved,
The Union that they loved they saved.

Our Hero Dead.

In such a cause who fears to die,
When he who fights for Freedom fights
For man, and those diviner rights
    Indulged him from on high ?

Name not his name ! It still must be
A thing of scorn and infamy.
Name not his name, but let him fly
    Far from the glorious strife,
And tell his fettered children why
    He hoards his little life !
Name not his name ! Unknown to fame,
    It shall not dwell upon the breeze :
But, blasted by the breath of shame,
    Shall fall beneath the centuries.

Name not his name ! No glowing verse
    Shall tell his deeds of glory o'er ;
But freeman's scorn and bondsman's curse
    Shall follow him forevermore,
These feared not death : they sought him, and
They met him boldly—sword in hand.

Our Hero Dead.

But, hold! The valor of your sires
No ornate song from me requires :
 Their country called—they went, they won :
They wrote their names on glory's page ;
And left their sons, for heritage,
 The soil they tread to-day upon !

But come ye here, for whom they bled,—
Bloom brightly flowers above their head !—
 Come from your cottages and halls!
 A son, or sire, or brother calls ;
And through their brother veterans' souls
To-day the one proud feeling rolls—
 Their country called—they went !
 So then, with one consent,
In Freedom's and in Honor's name,
In that of filial love and fame,
 Unveil their monument !

Boston, June, 1877.

BUNKER HILL.

The land was all in love to-day,
    Unknowing North, South, East, or West:
    To-night 'tis locked in peace and rest,
And all the continent is gay,
    And all the continent is blest.

Sing proudly, Stars of heaven, to-night!
    Shine brightly, spheres, that circle round,
    And flood the consecrated ground
With consecrated streams of light
    And consecrated waves of sound.

And, Northern maidens, floating near!—
    Oh, let your voices echo forth
    The golden gladness of the North
Into your Southern sisters ear—
    And make all melody and mirth!

And, soldiers of the Northern plumes,
    Thrice welcome bid each Southern band!
    One greeting from a brother's hand
Is worth ten thousand hero-tombs
    To any man in any land!

Bunker Hill, June 17, 1875.

Erin.

Here Ireland, stricken, begs for balms,
    For broken heart and bruised flesh;
Still shows the nail-prints in her palms
    And cries, being crucified afresh.

And, 'twixt the fools who hate her most,
    And those who hurt her most—her own,
She has but little left to boast
    Save strength to struggle on alone,

And courage still to persevere
    In what she holds her right divine,
And faith to feel that *some* New Year
    Shall see her star of promise shine:

And so it shall! The season hastes
    O Erin, when the last of woes
Shall come to thee, and all thy wastes
    Shall bloom and blossom as the rose!

January 1st, 1884.

Lyrics on Love.

Since Sappho,—She above
　　All poetesses
Who ever sang of love
　　Or love's caresses:

Since Sappho,—She who leapt,
　　Compelled by love, not duty,
Into the wave that wept
　　For joy to fold her beauty:

Since Sappho—I am next;
　　And, being as human,
I preach, and take for text
　　The love of woman.

THOU GOEST THY WAY.

Thou goest thy way, and I
    Another path pursue—
Beneath a drearier sky :—
'Tis well! and yet, I know not why,
    I weep to say adieu.

Yet shalt thou go thy way;
    For, though I love thee well
And fain would have thee stay,
I can in nothing say thee nay!—
    In nothing thou canst tell.

So little, loved one, go!
    A little longer here,—
A day or two below,—
And I shall meet thee, where they know
    No more the parting tear:

Where skies are ever fair;
    Where hearts are ever true ;
Where pain alone is rare;
Where Fate cannot divorce us, where
    We shall not say—adieu!

LOVE'S DECEASE.

Love died when we expected least
    That he would die; but, being dead,
Or tranced for burial, call the priest
    To read the rite that should be read
            Above his head!

Now scatter flowers upon his breast—
    The rarest, fairest flowers that grow,—
And take the heart that cannot rest
    Divorced from his, and let it go
            Still with him,—so!

And dig a grave in some dark dell,
    Remote, and lone, and hidden deep,
That no one passing by may tell
    Another—"There lies Love asleep!"
            Then none will weep.

BENEATH THE ROSES.

Full oft my thought, of late. Idelle,
  When bright the night-star burneth,
Unto the spot we loved so well
  In happier moments turneth:—
And to the time when there we sat
  By clambering roses shaded,
When still we talked of this, or that,
  Until the evening faded:

When still our laughter was not loud;
  When sadness was not sorrow;
When all our sky had not a cloud,
  Our day had not a morrow:
When love had never time for tears.
  Nay, knew not what their flow meant;
But ever drew the bliss of years
  From each succeeding moment.

Ay, oft remembrance of those days
  O'er sense and feeling flashes:
And though our vows have gone their ways,
  Though love be dust and ashes:
And though we woke from peace to pain—
  'Tis ever so, or mostly!—
I still would live life o'er again,
  Though it were twice as costly,

Could I but have thee by my side
  When night about me closes,
And clasp thee in my arms, my bride,
  For aye beneath the roses!

FORGIVE THEE:

Forgive thee? Though the years be long
　Since last I touched thy brow,
Men shall not say I wrought thee wrong
　Or broke my early vow
Won from me by one simple song,
　I must forgive thee now.

I do forgive thee, and I bless
　Thee as a dear regret,—
A golden, olden happiness
　That should be with me yet.
Forgive thee! I forgive thee, yes:
　Ask not that I forget!

REMEMBER THEE!

Remember thee! When I forget
   Myself, and all that has been mine,—
The moments more than precious yet,
   The nights you wont to call divine,—
When all that *is* hath ceased to be,
I then will cease to think of thee.

Still think of thee! When summer's sun
   Is wrapped in deep autumnal haze;
When every sphere its course hath run,
   And numbered its allotted days;
When sun and stars have ceased to be,
I then will cease to think of thee.

Remember thee! When love is nought;
   When truth is but an empty name:
When sorrow is the child of Thought,
   And sorrow's only offspring—shame:
When Love, Truth, Thought have ceased to be,
I then will cease—to think of thee!

THE DEFEAT OF LOVE.

" I go", said Love to his friends one day,
  "To a balmy island known to me,
To a happy island leagues away
  Set star-fair far in a Southern sea.

For there the mate that affection means
  To give my heart has waited long:
She calls—I go to those sweeter scenes
  Of life and love and summer and song.

Those sweeter scenes where the wild grape grows
  To thrill the throat of the land with wine:
Where all is sweet as is the rose
  To the bee that hangs to its heart divine!"

He built a boat of deep-sea-shell,
  Or meet for calm, or common gale;
He bade us all a kind farewell,
  Then took the tiller and spread the sail.

The Defeat of Love.

We watched him off—the wind blew free,
  Like electric spark he sped from the shore;
He crossed the bar; he won the sea ;
  Then night came down and closed him o'er.

　　　　　　＊　　　　＊　　　　＊　　　　＊

Well, days and weeks and months grew old,
  A year grew perfect and complete,
Ere to our ears the tidings rolled
  Of Love and Love's too dark defeat.

The maiden wearied of his delay,—
  For adverse grew both wind and tide,—
And said, " I will meet him on the way
  And guide him here!" She smiled in pride ;

For she was royal, and had ships
  And men to mark her least command :
And ere the word had left her lips,
  Her barge was ready to leave the land.

[over]

The Defeat of Love.

And she sailed Northward far and fast,
   And he sailed Southward steady and true :
They came together at length, *but passed*
   Each other one night, and neither knew.

So he sailed Southward o'er the main,
   And she sailed towards the Pole-star fair,
Till storms arose and wrecked them twain,
   And no one knows the when or where !

Ah, me! How often, or first or last,
   The lover and loved—the fitting two—
Have met on Life's large sea, and passed
   Each other forever, while neither knew !

TO ADELLE.

Though the hopes I have left be not many,
    I have one which is second to none,
A hope that is dearer than any,
    And it is—tho' this all may be ill or be well—
That perhaps, in the fairer Hereafter, Adelle,
    You and I will be one.

The streams which so tenderly blended
    To their ocean divided may run ;
But perhaps, when their course is all ended,
    Perhaps—tho' this all may be ill or be well—
Perhaps, in the vaster Hereafter, Adelle,
    The two may be one.

The days of affection have faded,
    The nights of our visions are gone ;
And we—we shall pass e'en as they did ;
    But perhaps—tho' this all may be ill or be well
Perhaps, in the mighty Hereafter, Adelle,
    You and I shall be one !

EPIMETHEUS.

The months fly by! November
  Is present with us now;
And why should I remember
  That early April vow?
Why longer should I long for,
  With tears and vain regret,
Or why still sigh in song for
  The days *thou* dost forget?

The season wanes; the flowers
  I placed upon thy head
Are withered with the hours,
  Are with them, ever dead.
And how should tender blossom
  Upon thee fresh remain,
When winter in thy bosom
  Doth hold eternal reign?

Epimetheus.

Or, now the year is dying,
   Why not, ere it be done,
Let all old love go flying
   After the old year's sun?
Why not give laugh for laughter,
   Shake hands and part with thought;
And love being asked for, after,
   Make answer—*Love was not?*

I will! no more I sorrow
   For that bright, brief, dear dream,
I launch my boat to-morrow
   Anew upon life's stream:
And let the breeze blow kindly,
   And let the tide run true,
Or let them both work blindly
   Their work, as weavers do:

Epimetheus.

And let my bark move quickly,
  Or be it slowly sped;
And let the stars gleam thickly,
  Or be they hid o'erhead—
I shall no more abandon
  My chart, but onward move,
No more to strike or strand on
  The rock of April love.

No, No! My soul's November
  Is here and with me now,
And I must not remember
  Again that sweet Spring-vow;
I must no longer long for,
  With tears and vain regret,
Nor sigh again in song for
  The days thou dost forget.

THOU HAST DONE IT—NOT I.

Thou hast done it, not I, yet I will not endeavor
   To dig the dear dead from the depths of the past ;
Let it slumber oblivion's slumber forever,—
   The book has been sealed—thou hast writ in it last !

Let it be as it is ! What is spoken is spoken—
   Entreaties are fruitless, apologies vain ;
For a thread in the web of Affection once broken,
   No art upon earth can unite it again.

I THOUGHT THAT TIME.

I thought that Time would teach me to forget;
    Yet years have passed since last I left thy side,
And thou art more than well remembered yet—
    My beautiful one—my bride!

I probe my thought and find the mystery lies
    In deeming love a merely temporal thing:
Whilst like a beam of light it floats and flies
    Upon a weariless wing.

JUNE.

O crimson-hearted, flower-producing June—
  Dear month of love, and laughter, and light song!
Wherein our mother brings her choral throng
  To hymn the hymns that sweetest are in tune:
Wherein all gaily goes save soul of wrong
  That takes to bed quite blinded by the light
  Of that sweet, sober, gentle queen of night
That rules the tides of earth and men—the moon;
  I love you! for it was beneath your skies
  I first looked love into her starry eyes:
I love you! for beneath your dome of blue
  I heard her answer—" And I love you too!"
I hate you!— mid your flowers it was my lot
To hear those same lips say—" I love you not!"

RELICS.

Put them aside—I hate the sight of them !—
 That golden wonder from her golden hair
 That faded lily which she once did wear
Upon her bosom—and that cold hard gem
 Which glittered on her taper finger fair.

They are of her, and, being so, they must
 Be like to her, and she is all a lie
 That seems a truth when truth is not a-nigh,—
A thing whose love is light as balance dust.
 I loved her once, I love— nay, put them by !

Conceal them like the dead from sight away !
 I must forget her and she was so dear
 In former times ! I could not bear them near :
Let them be sealed forever from the day—
 Be wrapt in darkness, shrouded—buried here

Where never more my eye may rest on them !
 This golden wonder from her golden hair—
 This faded lily that she once did wear
Upon her bosom—and this joyless gem
 That glittered on her taper finger fair.

AMORIS FINIS.

And now I go with the departing sun :
    My day is dead and all my work is done.
No more for me the pleasant moon shall rise
    To show the splendor in my dear one's eyes ;
No more the stars shall see us meet ; we part
    Without a hope, or hope of hope, at heart ;
For Love lies dead, and at his altar, lo,
Stands in his room, self-crowned and crested, — *Woe!*

FORGETTING.

Forgetting! Were forgetting
  Done easily as said,
I should not be regretting
  The days forever dead.

Forgetting ! Were it only
  Exertion of the will,
I should not be so lonely
  And sad so long, and still.

But who, in arms that folded
  The star-eyed, radiant Past,—
But who is he so moulded
  Can hold the present fast ;

And in this rapturous present
  Enwound, give never thought
To moments just as pleasant
  That were when these were not ?

FAREWELL !

Farewell!—a little word and light,
  Yet pregnant with regret to me ;
It seems a Saint Helena's height—
A mockery—to souls whose flight
  Hath been unto—what could not be !

Farewell!—I rest upon the word.
  It seems a solemn, saddening bell
At midnight in the tempest heard,
  A death-bed sigh—a funeral knell
That speaks of life and love interred,—
  It soundeth now—ah, sad!—Farewell !

IN DREAMS.

When disobedient Adam spurned
  An exile from his Eden came,
No doubt he sadly, daily turned
  And cursed the circling sword of flame :
And yet, perchance, when evening fell
  And stars came forth with pitying beams,
He slept and dreamed that all was well,—
  And walked his garden in his dreams.

So I, expelled from balmy bowers
  Through which 'twas once my joy to roam,
Awaking, curse the envious hours
  That hold me from my former home ;
And yet, sometimes, as night comes down,
  In dreams afar my spirit flies,—
I reassume my old renown,
  And lord again my Paradise !

TO MISS IASIGI.

Beloved! though the plume of wealth
  Cleaves to thee, clings,—even as a flower
Clings to its stem, until by stealth
  Of ill-bred breeze or sudden shower
Its hold and hope and heart and health
  Are broken in unhappy hour,—
I would resign Earth's proudest throne
  To call thee, having right, "mine own!"

Mine own!—to keep and have and hold,
  Mine own—my beauty—mine to bless;
To love, till love itself grow old,
  And the dark scythe-fiend's ruthlessness
Have put the gray above the gold;
Nay, even in death my love alone,—
Still loved, still lovely, still "mine own!"

To Miss Iasigi.

Mine! though Apollo's crimson car
   Wheels westward o'er the world, as well
As mine when night's sad, setting star
   Resigns his post of sentinel;
Mine own in time of peace—in war
   The hope on which my eye may dwell;—
My sun in shade, my shade in shine,
Forever and forever—mine!

Mine? Ah, alas! the barricade
   That Mammon rears between us twain
May not be overleaped, dear maid,
   Though high hearts break with parting pain.
The phantom passion must be laid;
   The harper taught another strain;
The knee must seek another shrine,
   For thou art not—*thou art not mine!*

Boston, 1880.

84

BON VOYAGE!

A pleasant journey o'er the rough
    Atlantic wave, with happy noons,
Auspicious evenings, and enough
    Of cloudless nights and milk-white moons!

A pleasant journey through the climes
    Of lore and love and sun and snow;
May all your times be summer times,
    And joy go with you as you go!

And when familiar to your ken
    Are Goth, and Greek, and Turk, and Russ,
And all the rest of them, why, then—
    A pleasant journey back to us!

A pleasant journey o'er the tide
    Of Time, where tempests oft prevail;
May friends be with you and abide
    And trade-winds take you as you sail!

And, lastly, I would wish you, Sweet!
    Beyond earth's utmost bounds and bars,-
Along that undiscovered street,—
    A pleasant journey to the stars!

January 2, 1884.

THE BEACON HILL COQUETTE.

" I am the truest marksman, I'm
   The surest shot beneath the sun!"
Said Love one day to Father Time,
   Whom he had chanced to hit upon.

" You are? Then," said the Reaper hoary,
   " Pick out your surest, subtlest dart,
And with its point prove me your story
   Upon that woman's heart!"

Love took the gauntlet up with glee,—
   For with the bow the boy was clever,—
And saying,—" Now, Sir, we shall see
   If I have idly boasted ever;

You know I made Olympian Jove
   Come down to earth to carry on his
Suit with Europa; then I drove
   My mother Venus to Adonis:

The Beacon Hill Coquette.

I set the chaste Moon, when the sun
   Was sleeping, all ablaze with passion,
So that she wooed Endymion,
   And won him, in right royal fashion :

I made Marc Antony let slip
   A world, power, glory, just to batter a
Swift moment at the dainty lip
   Of that dusk beauty Cleopatra :

I sent old Orpheus down to Hell
   To sing his spouse from o'er the river ;
And if I do not do as well
   To-day, my friend, I break my quiver ! "

So saying, he took good aim and flung :
   The arrow shot the sunshine gaily,—
It missed ; the target turned unstung
   And questioned—if he *practised daily* ?

The Beacon Hill Coquette.

Love flung his slender bow away,
 And catching Time, who had not waited,
Laid hold upon him, crying—" Pray,
 When was that wondrous one created ?

I have been lounging late in climes
 Where maids are soulful, songful, sunny ;
Where hearts are musical as rhymes
 Anacreon-lipt, and sweet as honey ;

Is she of some new order plann'd
 While I have carelessly been straying ?
Or is she of some loveless land
 Where never went a sunbeam playing ? "

" Poor Cupid ! " answered Father T—,
 " I will enlighten you ; but yet
It is a sacred secret,—she
 Is but a Beacon-hill coquette ! "

I SAW YOUR BEAUTY.

I saw your beauty ripe and rare,
  Your Attic face and sensuous form,
But found them framed for seasons fair—
  Not winter days, or nights of storm.

I might have loved, did I not know
  That breast, though all devoid of sin,
Though pure without as polar snow,
  Was cold as polar snow within.

I could have loved you, but a face
  Came evermore betwixt us twain
To win me from your art and grace
  Back to my better self again.

I would have loved you, could the bliss
  Her presence gave me be forgot;
But, as it was, remember this:
  I loved you not—I loved you not!

MY SOUTHERN NIGHTS.

Ah, me! my Southern nights! my nights beside
  The sighing, sobbing, soulful, sunny sea
With my dear love!—my love magnificent-eyed
  As she who trod on power for Antony,—
  As that great queen all queen and more to me,
In that she bartered stroke for stroke with Fate,
  And dared to die—ere bend a plaintive knee ;
Or as that other who did one time wait
The whole night through beside the Trojan gate.

Memorial moments—all too swiftly sped !
  Memorial nights—departed all too soon !
When delicate fires were fainting overhead
  In the voluptuous presence of the moon ;
  And breezes, laden with the scent of June,
Unto love's whisper answered with a sigh ;—
  Prophetic prelude of the saddest tune
That ever broke a heart, or dimmed an eye !—
And Araby's perfumes on drowsy wing went by.

I CANNOT KISS THIS STRANGER.

I cannot kiss this stranger yet,
   Nor yet espouse it in the stead
   Of one—the lovely one and dead—
Whom I may nevermore forget :—

Of one who gave me second birth,
   And reconciled me to my clay ;
   I cannot kiss it yet—to-day !
And keep it at its vaunted worth.

'Twould seem like sacrilege to fold
   My heart about another form,
   While even a memory is warm
Of that—which but so late grew cold.

THE DREAMS THAT HAVE FADED.

I may love thee forever, but nevermore—never
   Can love make us one as it once made us one ;
Whate'er the Fates find us, the Past is behind us,
   And naught can undo now the thing that is done.

Though Time treat us kindly, or buffet us blindly,
   Though stars shine above us or blessings no more,
We cannot forget them, we still must regret them—
   The dreams that have faded—the days that are o'er !

APART.

Yes, love of mine, and fair as any fair—
　　Song of my soul, and soul of all this song !
I will forgive thee, though thou makest bare
　　And bleak my life :—yea, by thy glorious hair
And violet eyes, I will forgive the wrong.

I will forgive thee, even as I expect
　　To be forgiven of all my own ill deeds
By Him who holds all people His elect,—
　　Who judges kindly, caring not for creeds.

I do forgive ! Albeit it hurts the heart
　　To say—It might have been !—still o'er and o'er :
To ask, yet find no aid in any art,
To know that we must walk life's ways apart —
　　O lovelessness of love !—for evermore.

APEROTOS.

It may be true—it may be true!
　But is it not a weary thing
To wave alone a joyless wing?
　To have no love to glad us through
Our long and lonely journey, round
　The many spheres that we must greet,
Ere yet, with hallowed hands and feet,
　We touch upon celestial ground.

Ah, yes! It may be best to be
　Without a taint of love or touch
In all your blood; but I am such
　That loveless life were death to me:
And death— so it had love to fill
　The pauses in the music—were
Not half so bad, not half so bare,
　Since, loving,—I am living still.

TO ISABEL.

My sweet fastidious Isabel,
   Thy silence hath been read!
I shall not sigh to say farewell,—
   'Tis sometimes lightly said;
Albeit it soundeth like a knell
   O'er days forever dead.

Amid the beautiful and bright
   Somewhere upon this earth
Affection may sometime alight
   On one of equal birth,
With face more fair than thine to-night
   And heart of higher worth.

And I may cleave to her, and she
   May cast her lot with mine :
No shadow on our hearth shall be,—
   There *may* be none on thine :
And I shall never weep for thee,
   Nor pale for thee, nor pine.

LURLINE.

We know the thing you were, Lurline!
  As cold as care; but you were fair,
And being worshipped as a Queen,
  Young Harold fell into your snare,
  Although we warned him to beware
Your Arctic smile and marble mien!

We know the river, too, Lurline!
  Its wave was cold, but he was bold,
And little paused to think, I ween,
  How bitter, black and fierce it rolled—
  So he should never more behold
Your Arctic smile and marble mien!

THOU ART LIKE EARTH.

Thou art like Earth who saw the sun, and said :
　Behold the faithless thing I deemed so true!
It lately warmed me, now its warmth is fled,—
　It scarcely viewed me till it passed from view!

To which the Sun replied: Here am I still
　Where thou hast left me; here will I remain ;
And here, forsooth, my stay shall be, until
　The law of Nature turns thee back again!

And when the law compelled her, and She came,
　She found him older, in all else—the same.

SONG.

I know not if it be her eyes,
   Outshining all the stars that rise
With their deep splendor calm and true,
   That makes me love her as I do:
The only thing that I can tell
Is that I love her—wondrous well!

I cannot name the separate charm
   Of ankle, eye, or lip, or arm,
That charms me; I can only say
   My love increases day by day;
That, more than tongue of mine can tell,
I love her, love her—wondrous well!

LOVE.

TO ———

Love much resembles daybreak; none can say
    When it begins, or when it terminates;
It comes and passes like a dream away:
Perhaps the common friendships of to-day
    May form to-morrow's loves, or next day's hates.
    Who waits for love, is loving while he waits;
Who sneers at love, is loving while he sneers;
    Who fears to love, is loving while he fears.
All men, all women love: even I, who speak,
    I find I am a swimmer far from shore;
My soul is dizzy and my limbs are weak:
    Say, shall I sink, or strive a little more?
Why should I strive, when love will have its will?
I hate to love, and yet—I love thee still.

A WELCOME.

I welcome thee, dear one, with kisses
    From harvest fields,—
I welcome thee back from the blisses
    The country yields.

I welcome thee back from the flowers
    Dew-fed and fair,
Where the moments are mirth, and the hours
    Are woven of air.

Where sweetest of singers are singing
    Fresh songs and sweet:
Where all things seem banded in bringing
    One joy complete.

I welcome thee, now that the summer
    Departing smiles:
I welcome thee back as a comer
    From balmy isles:—

A Welcome.

From isles that are history-haunted
    In vale and hill;
Whose atmospheres are enchanted
    And holy still.

I welcome thee, holding it duty
    To prove my own
Soul-summer as full of all beauty
    As thine—just flown;

My summer, that follows in wake of
    Thy summer sere:
I welcome thee! come and partake of
    It all the year!

THEN- AND NOW.

Not even a glance to say that I am seen !
  Not even a glance from that soft starry eye—
  Not even a glance ! God knows the reason why !
I surely cannot be what I have been,
  Or, sweet, you would not pass unheeding by,
Even were I vassal and yourself my queen ;
  Nor would you hold your sunny head so high.
For I would bend it with the weight of love
  That I should shower upon it : I would bring
Your heart to read in every star above
  Your name with mine entwined as queen and king,—
Lords of the earth, of love, of time, of fate—
Supreme of all things being or small or great—
  Yea, lords of love—so lords of everything !

New York, Oct., 1879.

WE MET—WE PARTED.

To———

We met—we parted : common ties
    No longer link us each to each :
The future all before us lies,
    The past is all beyond our reach.

We met—we parted : 'tis an old
    And time-worn tale : and yet to me
It seemeth wonderful to hold
    A path that is unknown to thee.

Could I but be the thing thou art,
    Or rather that thou seem'st to be—
A thing of dull or deadened heart
    I deem it might be well for me.

We Met — We Parted.

Could I, as thou hast done, forget
  The pleasure and the promise flown,
I should not be as I am yet—
  A creature desolate and lone.

But, ivy-like, I ever climb
  The closer to the shattered wall:
Thus sadness mars my every rhyme,
  My chaplet dark is cypress all.

And as I strive to break the spell
  That links to sadness song and soul.
I ever hear the "passing-bell,"--
  My chime is but --a funeral toll !

IS IT MY FATE?

TO————

Is it my fate,—a trifle worse,
  Perhaps, than fates of most men are,—
Some mystic and peculiar curse
  Inseparable from my star?

Or is it, for I have been wild
  In youth, although I wished none ill,
That Love, at which I one time smiled,
  Must prove herself revengeful still?

Or is it,—but thy lips are dumb,
  Thy lips hot with my kisses yet,
That love became too burdensome
  For thee to bear as amulet?

Or art thou false? If this be so,
  Then I, until these pulses cease
To answer to the red blood's flow
  Will never take the hand of peace.

For if it be that in the deep
  Of thy clear eye such thing is found
As falsehood,—then let Virtue weep,—
  For truth is not where earth is round!

January, 1883.

TRUE LOVE AND TRIED.

A RONDEL.

True love and tried that never sleeps,
  Though all the world may sleep beside :
But still perpetual vigil keeps —
  True love and tried !

Whatever comes with time or tide,—
  Whoever sows—whoever reaps, —
Still faithful will this love abide.

Yea, more ! Beyond the purple steeps,
  Beyond the river's margin wide,
We yet shall know thine utmost deeps,
  True love and tried !

BY THE FOUNTAIN.

By the margin of the fountain in the soulful summer
  season,
   While the song of silver-throated singers smote and
     shook the air,
While the life seemed sweet enough to live without a
   ray of reason
   Save that it was, and that the world was lovely
     everywhere.

By the fountain,—where the Oreads, through the moon-
   lit nights enchanted
   Of the summer, may have sported and have laved
     their shining limbs :
By the fountain,—which in elder days the Mœnads may
   have haunted,
   Giving all the praise to Bacchus. twining wreaths
     and singing hymns :

By the Fountain.

By the fountain whose pellucid waves within the deli-
cate basin
  Daintily tinkling, dropping dreamily, made a music
    in the ears
Like the echo of some high, some arch-angelic diapason
  Drifting downward from the ever swinging never si-
    lent spheres:

By the fountain fringed with laurel, whose green
branches, intertwining,
  Let but few swift shafts of sunshine in to paint the
    odorous space,
Lo! a maiden fairer far than any future lay reclining
  On an arm whose white, warm beauty shot a splendor
    through the place.

Oh, her eyes were like to Leda's lights divine to him
who misses
  In a desert land his pathway when the moon is on the
    wane;
And her tress was dark as Vashti's, and her lips were
  ripe for kisses,
  Though on them had fallen no kiss as yet of passion
    or of pain.

And her smile was bright and splendid as the east
 when morn is breaking,
  Only softer far and sweeter, far diviner and more
   calm,
And her voice was like the song of birds the sylvan
 echoes waking
  In the gardens of a king where gleam the myrtle and
   the palm.

Then the blood that fed my pulses leaped to life as if
 Apollo
  Had recrossed the March meridian, bringing winter
   in his track,
And my heart made merry music, while the streamlet
 in the hollow
  Did its very best to answer with a hopeful echo back.

Then the poet and the lover leaped to life and wrought
 within me,
  Who 'neath many a constellation had been but a man
   to men :—
Who had knelt before the altars and the fanes that failed to win me
  From reproachings and repinings to my better self
   again.

SHALL THIS, TOO, FAIL ME?

Shall this, too, fail me ? Shall
   This swift-grown love, and sweet,
Be doomed to fade and fall
   In ruins at my feet ?

Shall evermore eclipse
   Succeed to dim my star ?
Shall all fruit of my lips
   Prove fruit of Istakhar ?

Is love a trifle, then ?
   Is woman's truth and trust
Become a thing that men
   May trample in the dust ?

And have we merely met
   To dream, and wake, and part—
With an immortalized regret
   Inhabiting each heart ?

CONSISTENCY.

A SONNET.

In the orient of our love, when all was bright,
  Ere youth's sweet sunshine faded from the heart
As from the cheek,—ere ever came the night
  That comes to all, when men dispel in part
The darkness gathering over them with light
  That is not light, or is the light of art,—
Ere love is drowned in wine, thou bad'st me swear
  That I would never love save thee alone :
  I swore, but made (of course in undertone)
A saving clause, to love none else—less fair.
But now when we are old—for time has flown—
  I may as well confess how then I lied.
  But think not thou, though distance may divide,
My love hath changed!—I love thee, and—alone !

  1879.

MY LIFE.

All for a luckless love—
    A boyish blunder—
The heaven keeps black above,
    As Earth is under!

Tost like a leaf by the wind
    In the winter weather;
Tost by a Power unkind
    Hither and thither!

Tost as a weed on the tide
    Of a shoreless ocean!
No haven wherein to hide—
    Eternal motion!

No knowledge of whither bound—
    My courage failing:
Darkness and mist around—
    Eternal sailing!

New York, Oct., 1879.

It must have been a strange spectacle to see the "in futuro" author of the Vicar of Wakefield and Citizen of the World strolling through Europe scraping an existence out of a diseased and dilapidated violin. But this is a world of anomalies. Strange things have grown familiar.—G. F. C.

WHAT NEW FOUND PAIN IS THIS?

What new found pain is this—
   So cutting, keen of edge?
It seems there was a Judas-kiss
   And is a broken pledge.

What pain? 'Tis like all pain
   On earth of woman born,
It soon will go; and I again
   Laugh love and it to scorn.

It soon will die, and yet
   I would it were not she
Who gave it birth!—but I forget,
   She is nothing now to me.

She won my heart, and wore—
   To please her woman wit—
It for a day, or something more,
   And then discarded it.

And can I pardon this,
   Nor from my manhood fall,—
The broken vow, the love, the kiss?—
   I will forget them all.

CURSED BE THE BIGOTRY.

Cursed be the bigotry which thus can tear
    Asunder those who love !   And doubly cursed
Be they who Nature's order have reversed
    And made life's burden hard indeed to bear !
    Why must I wear the gyves these choose to wear ?
Why must I kiss the rod these choose to kiss ?
Why must I call that bliss which is no bliss ?
    Why in an unrewarded labor share ?
I loathe the Egyptian flesh-pots ; I defy
    The purpled Pharaohs, and their vaunted power—
Their chariots and their horsemen ; yea, and I
    Will still defy them to my latest hour !
Believing in the end 'twill all be well,—
For Nature knows and guides her chosen Israel.

WOULD I DRINK IT?

Would I drink it—the cup of the beautiful Eld?
  Tho' it saddened my heart, tho' it maddened my
    brain,
I would hold it on high as I formerly held,
  And drink it, and drink it again and again.

I would live yet awhile in the days which are dreams,—
  I would look on the star that illumined my path,—
I would quaff from the bowl which was bright as its
    beams,—
  Though to-morrow I knew it the Marah of wrath.

THE COMMON FATE.

I need not ask the reason why
    Thy love is given and loveliness
To one who loves thee less than I,—
    Yea, less than I—far less!

Nor need I argue that it is
    Of human wisdom or divine,
That thou art given to him for his,
    And not to me for mine.

Nor will I envious rail at him
    Who broke my dream half-dreamed, and stole—
To wear until its beauties dim —
    The bright crown-jewel of my soul.

Nor can I blame thee : hardly thou
    Could'st ever guess the love I bore :
For scarce I knew thee, ere a vow
    Had made thee his forevermore.

Oh, 'tis of life the common law—
    It is in love the common fate—
That man at length should say—"I saw!"
    Then sigh—"*but saw too late!*"

MY LOVE-COMPELLING LOVE.

My love-compelling Love, my more than friend,
  My dream by night, my thought the whole day long!—
  If there be aught of beauty in my song,
It is because my soul to thine doth tend :
That thine from out its fulness still doth lend
  To mine a part of its particular grace
As mystic as the motions of the spheres,
  Which keep their course in yonder azure space
And fling on earth the measure of the years.
All things are lovely ever in the light
  Of lovely eyes.   Perchance 'tis thus thou see'st
  From thine own crimson chamber of the east
Down in my vale, where all to me is night,
Shoot through the shadows thick one shaft with radi-
    ance bright.

THOU ART MY FRIEND?

Thou art my friend? 'tis well—my star ascends!
　　Few had I since the moment of my birth;
Nor thought I e'er to say—"We two are friends!"
　　To aught that wears the livery of earth.

I have had idols,—friends I called them then,—
　　But Dagon-like they sought their native dust:
I deemed them gods, and found them only men:
　　I deemed them kind,—they were not even just!

Friendship depends upon a brittle thread,
　　Whose strands wear bravely in the summer days;
But when the winter comes, and cold and dread,
　　When Fortune sheds no more his genial rays,—
When cloud and storm appear, the fabric soon decays.

Thou Art My Friend?

And need I say I loved?—Thou know'st it well :
  How well I loved thou dost not need to know.
And need I say my castle faery fell,
  Or speak of those who joyed to see it low?—
I might have turned and answered blow for blow.

I left them to themselves, nor chose to fan
  The flame of anger into further glow :
I think, although that was no portion of their plan,
  They made the poet—when they marred the man !

"AWAY FROM ME."

The beach sighed for the sea when it had lost it,—
  Sighed for the sea it deemed too rude a sea,—
When from its breathing bosom forth it tost it,
  Proud crying—"Away from me!"

"So be it, dear beach!" the sad wave said, receding:
  "The time shall come when it shall come to pass
That you shall cry, and I shall hear, unheeding,
  'Away from me, alas!'"

And here, dear maiden, may you find a moral:
  Think—ere you spurn true men for butterflies;
Think—ere you slaughter in a needless quarrel
  Life's opportunities!

Judge not by looks, but by immortal merit:
  Worth dwells forever in the hidden parts;
And oft the roughest-seeming ones inherit
  The very noblest hearts.

Pause—ere you turn to dearth and dust and ashes
  A love divine, by bidding it go free!
So that you cry not, late, with wet eyelashes,
  "Alas!—away from me!"

Tybee Island, Georgia.

IS THERE A GOD?

Is there a God, then, above us?
 I ask it again and again:
Is there a good God to love us—
 A God who is mindful of men?

Is there a God who remembers
 That we have our nights as our noons?
Our dark and our dismal Decembers
 As well as our garden-gay Junes?

New York, Oct., 1879.

IS THE GOD?

Is the God, then, deaf, that man
   Cries ever from depths of pain
Till his soul is sick, and his heart is wan,
   And ever cries in vain?

Is the God, too, dumb, that He
   Deigns signal nor reply
To any supplication we
   Address to Him on high?

New York, Oct., 1879.

TO A COQUETTE.

What though your lips be ripe and rare,
  And royal in their curve for kisses?
What though your eyes, too, do their share,
  And shoot a shaft that seldom misses?

What though your cheeks be ruby-red,
  And draw our sense like rich June-roses;
When, for a maiden's heart, 'tis said,
  Within your breast a flirt's reposes?

Reposes? Yea, the very word!
  For, from its silences and slumbers
Nor song of bard, nor voice of bird,
  Nor Love, nor music's noblest numbers,

To a Coquette.

Nor anything that ever was
    Of good, or glad, or high, or holy,
Hath warmed or waked it to applause,
    Nor anything I know but Folly.

Yet, mark me! it will sometime wake,—
    How strong soe'er you wish to numb it,
And, rousing to its new self, shake
    The ashes of its old self from it :—

Will sometime wake, will sometime speak,
    Unheeding all your sensual hushes,
And prophesy that even *your* cheek
    Shall part with all its blooms, and blushes :

And tell you that your eye shall lose
    Its lightning and your lip its beauty :
And make you weep you did not choose
    To find your friends in Truth and Duty.

PASSION.

As when the wildfire sweeps o'er prairie wide,
   Devours the nettle choking up the way,
Breathes on the lily nodding there in pride
   And turns its plume to darkness and decay :

So o'er the soul the flame of passion goes,
   Destroys the hideous and alike the fair,—
Alike the rankest weed, the rarest rose,—
   And leaves alone a waste of ashes there.

WHY FRUITLESSLY MOURN WE?

Why fruitlessly mourn we—why chafe with our chain?
   Know we not link by link every chain will decay?
Why weep we in sorrow, why shrink we in pain?
   These things pass away.

Why thus do the noblest created despair?
   The ill as the good hath its "go" as its "stay;"
For the good and the ill and the foul and the fair
   Shall all pass away.

And the hope and the fear and the care and the toil
   Are but threads woven into the mantle of clay,
And alike being Time and Oblivion's spoil
   Shall all pass away.

BRING A FITTING SHROUD!

Bring a fitting shroud for the moments fled—
  The moments of music and mirth which were mine:
Ah, what shall cover my beautiful dead
  But a fabric of moments as fair and as fine.

Bring a fitting shroud for the love now fled,
  The love ever faithless, yet wondrously fair:
Ah, what can cover my treacherous dead
  Save the heart which was warm and is cold with it
    there!

'TIS STRANGE, YOU THINK.

'Tis strange, you think, that I remember yet
  The word, the kiss, the parting place, the date,
When Love fell dead before the feet of Fate?
  Strange? It were strange indeed, did I forget.

The moon was westward, and her upper rim
  Was barely visible o'er the mountain head;
Hand locked in hand we stood, and then you said
  Even as she set and all the land grew dim : —

"I wonder will this love of ours set so,
  And all our lives grow dark, and cold, and drear,
With but a star-beam floating there and here?"
  And then you shuddered, and I answered—"No."

And yet I know not how it came to be—
  Half fault perhaps of yours, half fault of mine,
We parted there amid the laurestine;
  And with you anger went, regret with me.

You cherished anger—I espoused regret :
  And as the moon now sets behind the hills,
Through every vein the ancient memory thrills.
  That was the time—ah, how could I forget!

NAY, I MAY NEVER LOVE AGAIN!

Nay, I may never love again!—
   Love is for children, not for men :
It is a measureless abyss,
   O'er arched with many a faithless kiss :
It is a rainbow based on gloom,
   A lily waving o'er a tomb ;—
The Muse might almost take her oath
   'Tis Scylla and Charybdis both.

MY MARRIAGE MORNING.

Like that wild gladness warriors feel
   In warriors who have carven a name,
With their own hands and subtle steel,
   Upon the rock of Fame.

Or nobler joy that poets know
   When from the brain where seemed a dearth
   Of thoughts, of things, of wit and worth,
Spring thoughts that glint and gleam and glow
   And gladden all the earth :—

Like that—all earthly joys above,
   This sweetest pain beneath the skies
Which comes with the first kiss of love,
   And with it lives and dies.

My Marriage Morning.

The clouds go by, and the new morrow breaks
  In beauty bright above the happy hills;
The throstle warbles and the west-wind shakes
  The shining daffodils.

And all the flowers—the fair ones and the rare—
  Dance now that all the dusk and dark is done;
Drink in the dew, scent the delicious air,
  And mock the morning sun.

And, oh! my heart,—that also knew the night,
  With cold moons gleaming and few stars above,—
Wakes from its dreaming to the day's delight,
  Kist into life by love!

Yea, all my soul, impatient of the dusk,
  Forsakes despair—its former chrysalis,—
And, taking new wings, leaves its ancient husk
  To crumble at a kiss!

Millhaven, Ont., August 22nd, 1883.

131

A QUESTION.

They say that disembodied friends
   Do sometimes hover round us here,
And smooth our ways, and form our ends
   To suit the ever circling year
That with their coming ever blends.

If so, the friend I loved hath now
   Improved the motion of my days
And scattered round my burdened brow
   A few celestial-seeming rays;—
Relit my lamp—I know not how—

From his own sphere of happiness,
   From his own orb of dear delight,
And swept a moment my distress
   Into its native realm of night,—
Into its native nothingness.

But shall my sorrow come no more?
   And shall I find an endless rest
When my sad star hath vanished o'er
   The mist-girt mountains of the west
To shine upon another shore?

TRUE LOVE.

True love can never alter,—
   True love can never die:
False love alone can falter,—
   False love alone can fly.

Love, darling, needs to borrow
   No beauty of the morn
Through day to the to-morrow
   It smiles with scorn on scorn:

On hate—but devils only
   Can hate—it ever glows:
True love leaves no heart lonely
   It glads where'er it goes.

Even through the dust and ashes
   Of hope wet by sad tears
It flings a flame which flashes
   Athwart the coming years.

Aye, as the wild years flying
   For swiftness lose their breath,
It goes with them, in dying
   It takes the hand of death.

Written September, 1885—a few days before his death. So also the following pieces, the last of which was found in his pocket after death.—C. J. C.

FIRST LOVE.

Ah, love is deathless ! we do cheat
    Ourselves who say that we forget
Old fancies : last love may be sweet,
    First love is sweeter yet.

And day by day more sweet it grows
    Forevermore, like precious wine,
As Time's thick cobwebs o'er it close,
    Until it is divine.

Grows dearer every day and year,
    Let other loves come, go at will :
Although the last love may be dear,
    First love is dearer still.

Sept. 1885.

ALL I ASK.

Wherefore should I play the lover?
    What care I for blushing bride?
All I ask when all is over
    Is to sleep by mother's side.

Sept. 1885.

STANDING ON TIPTOE.

Standing on tiptoe ever since my youth
   Striving to grasp the future just above,
I hold at length the only future—Truth,
   And Truth is Love.

I feel as one who being awhile confined
   Sees drop to dust about him all his bars :—
The clay grows less, and, leaving it, the mind
   Dwells with the stars.

Sept 1885.

ADELPHI.

Fraternal love and truth and honor gone?
All faith divorced from life?   If this be so
Man's star sinks westering, and the world he walks—
Untouched of any ray of future hope,
Past all redemption, dead indeed in sin,
Bearing the burden of the primal curse,
Reels on to ruin, and her ancient dusk—
Wheels through the darkness to her final time!
But is this so?   I think it were in me
The veriest heresy to hold it so,
When I, not seeking, stumble once, ev'n once
In a whole lifetime, on a love like that
Of Edgar, and of Albert Henderson—
A love beyond the love of woman's love,
A love beyond the love of woman far.

Two brothers, one is living still—from him
I heard the story,—Edgar Henderson,
And Albert, older by a year or two,
Loved one, and the same maiden, Minna Vane,
The toast, and boast of all the country round,
As fair as starlight, sweet as summer morn
In tropic isles, and pure and good withal.
She was their cousin, and from infancy
Had dwelt beside them, mingled in their sport
Whilst they were children, and when they had grown
To manhood, in their sober studies joined,
Till she became (and not unconsciously)
A part and portion of the life of each,
While they in turn became as dear to her.

To neither brother gave she preference;
Or, if she preference gave, it was not marked;
And if she preference had, she told it not.
When Edgar saw that Albert loved the girl
He would not speak to hurt his brother's hope;
When Albert saw that Edgar also loved
He would not throw a pebble in his way;
When Minna saw that she was loved by both,
Not dreaming wrong she fed them both on love.

Yet envy never crept between them ; they
Were formed of proud material in the which
No dross was mixed.   They only wrangled thus.
(In hall or hunt, an ever ready theme,
Which made all others servant to itself) :
" Now Edgar go to Minna, make her yours,
She loves you vastly ; you have but to call
And down the bird will flutter to your hand."
And thus :   " Nay, Albert, you who love her most,
And are the elder, as the better man,
You shall go to her ; you shall make her yours."
Each chided each so twenty times a day,
And were it forty times 'twere all the same,
Each loved his brother more than his desire.

Once Albert sought and asked her secretly.
" Do you love Edgar, cousin—yea or nay ?"
But she made answer with a rose-red blush,
(Which Albert might interpret as he would),
" I love you both !"   And Edgar also went,
Unknown to Albert, and desired to know
Whether she loved his brother ; but the maid
Replied as ever, " I do love you both !"

And when he fain would press her harder still
For certain knowledge, in her woman-way
She led him on to talk of other things,
Till he forgot his mission, and went home
Wise as he was the day before he asked.
So many suns set circling, many moons
Increased and waned, three summers came and went,
And still the matter doubtful hung in court.

But when the fourth year opened Edgar said,
"See, brother! full three years are dead and gone,
And Minna sends all others from her side,
Awaiting one of us; you will not go
To speak her, nor will I alone, now let
Us go together, hand in hand, and say,
'We love you, cousin, each of us, so choose
Which one of us will add you to his joys.
By your decision, be it what it may,
We pledge our honor we shall rest content.'"
And Albert rose and cried, "So be it then!"
And forth they went and bade her take her choice.
Then she, sweet Minna, of the golden hair
And perfect form and face and starry eyes,

Said only ever when they came to her,
Being weak, desiring but not knowing right,
" Agree between yourselves,—I love you twain ;
By your decision, be it this or that,
I pledge my maiden faith I will abide."
Now had she spake in other wise, and said,
When Albert came—" I love your brother !"—then
Edgar had won her ; or when Edgar asked
Had she, " I love your brother Albert ! " said,
Albert had had her : but " I love you twain :
Go, settle the affair between yourselves,
And I by your decision will abide."
Perplexed them much, and they could not agree.

And so another year was born of Time,
Was stricken with extreme old age and died,
And slumbered with his parents of the past,
While Minna knew not who should be her lord.
But when the second summer closed its buds
And on each calyx prest a parting kiss ;
When Autumn came with cooler winds and showers,
And lowering clouds foreboding Winter's reign ;
When late green leaves were tinting to their fall,

Adelphi.

And Northern birds were looking towards the South
And sighing for its suns and genial fruits,
Breaking the seal of silence from his lip,
" For the last time, my brother, she is yours,
So answer, will you wed her—yes or no ?"
Said Albert.   " She is *yours*," was the reply,
" For you her heart hath waited many days ;
For you she puts all other suitors by ;
For you she hoards the honey of her lip,
Wooed, as you know, by many a vagrant bee ;
For you she hopes to wear her orange wreath ;

Now, this being so (and well I know it is),
I pray you, by the love you have for her,
And by the love I have for her, make not
A winter of her life, as you will do
Not taking her unto your heart, for see !
Being fixt, beyond all change, or chance of change,
I swear I will not wed her whilst you live ;
And, swearing, wish you three score years and ten ;
Nay, more, so that they be not burdensome,
A golden age with golden joys annexed :
Nor think that I will envy you your bliss,—
That she will be my sister is enough."

Then Albert leaned his head upon his hands,
And knit his brow, and bit his nether lip,
As if he rolled the matter to and fro,
Which Edgar marking, thought " He yields at length,
And he will wed her ;" but he knew him not,
Albeit he was the brother of his soul.
At length, " Well, leave me for an hour alone :
An hour ere this hath settled weightier things :
An hour shall loose, or cut, this Gordian knot.
Come at its close, your answer will be here."

Then Edgar, with a laugh upon his lip,
And yet another rippling round his heart,
Rejoicing in the sacrifice he made,
And quaffing in anticipation from
A cup of joy he thought should soon be full,
To Minna went and told her all was well,
They having settled it in quiet wise.
But scarcely had the word fall'n from his tongue,
When one came to him running. Calling him
Aside, with trembling speed, he told his tale :

" You had but left the Park when Albert came
Into the armory, biting at his beard,
And muttering ever strangely through its maze,
Not dreaming I was watching him the while—
' It is the only way, the only way,
And being the only way it is the best.'
Plucked from its rest a rapier, and ere I
Divined his purpose sheathed it—in himself.
I ran, and caught, and laid him down, when he
With gentlest smile said, ' Maurice, you are late.
It was the only way, the only way;
Tell Edgar 'twas the only way, and best,
And tell him that I loved him to the last,
Far more than life, and more than my desire ;
And tell him farther, 'twas my will and wish,
And he will work it seeing it is my last,
That he should wed his cousin.'   Here the blood,
Which left his wound, as water leaves its fount,
Choked other utterance, and he drooped his head,
And with your name half-spoken, gasped and died."

Then Edgar, groping as a blind man might,
And bending 'neath the burden of the blow,

The bitter burden of a new found pain,
Walked through the stillness of the starry night,
And through the giant shadows of the elms,
Unto his home and knew it all too true.
With funeral rite, but naught of pageantry,
Albert was laid to slumber with his sires,
And Edgar sorrowed for him many days,
And Minna sorrowed with him for her friend :
And when the accustomed time of mourning passed—
(Albeit he mourned him ever in his heart,)
Holding his dying wish in due respect,
He went to Minna, none his rival now,
And took her to his heart and hearth and home,
To love and cherish her forevermore
As one who had been purchased with a price.

Such is the story as it came to me,
Nor wrapt, nor woven in cunning word or phrase,
But unadorned, unvarnished, simply clad.
It may not cap your confidence in man,
Nor rivet fast your mind to that *I* hold,
But yet I hold, above the voice of all,

Though thrice a thousand rise denying it,
That noble faith is not divorced from life,
That love fraternal still abides on earth,
And I do hope to hold it—to the end !

He told his story, and a pause ensued ;
Such pause as comes between the levin's light
And the rough-throated thunder crash ; such pause
As waters seem to make, the rapid reached,
Before they take the leap and jar the air
And fling the spray of their wild agony
Full in his face who ventures near to them :—
Such pause befel. Then burst a babble forth
Of many voices, as at Babel's tower,
And every listener stood a critic crowned,
Self-crowned as any critic, and self-made,
And ready each at his own altar base
To slay the poet who had dared to slay
Their hate of love and the high heart of man.

Lyrics in Pleasant Places

AND

Other Places.

"AH, ME! THE MIGHTY LOVE —"

Ah, me! the mighty love that I have borne
  To thee, sweet Song! A perilous gift was it
My mother gave me that September morn
  When sorrow, song, and life were at one altar lit.

A gift more perilous than the priest's: his lore
  Is all of books and to his books extends;
And what they see and know he knows—no more,
  And with their knowing all his knowing ends.

A gift more perilous than the painter's: he
  In his divinest moments only sees
The inhumanities of color, we
  Feel each and all the inhumanities.

1885.

WISDOM—A SONNET.

Wisdom immortal from immortal Jove
    Shadows more beauty with her virgin brows
Than is between the pleasant breasts of Love
    Who makes at will and breaks her random vows,
And hath a name all earthly names above :
The noblest are her offspring ; she controls
    The times and seasons—yea, all things that are—
The heads and hands of men, their hearts and souls,
    And all that moves upon our mother star,
And all that pauses 'twixt the peaceful poles.
Nor is she dark and distant, coy and cold,—
    But all in all to all who seek her shrine
In utter truth, like to that king of old
Who wooed and won—yet by no right divine.

DOWNS AND UPS.

Dance of moonlight on summer waves,
  Drip of streamlet and dip of oar;
Echo softly singing in caves,
  Grounding keels on a shining shore:

Laboring ships on wintry seas,
  Clamorous feet upon slimy decks;
Drowning shrieks on an angry breeze,
  Mangled corpses and tangled wrecks:

Music and laughter and love and song,
  Violets, roses, and lilies white;
Beautiful forms in a moving throng,
  Perfume and wine and a gala night.

Downs and Ups.

A pale, worn face in an attic lone,
  Bending over a wretched bed,
A clasp of hands, a dying moan,
  The rattle, the hush—and a spirit fled!

Golden prospects and ominous clouds;
  Impassable walks and level drives;
Glittering silks and colorless shrouds;
  Flattering records, and shattered lives:

Brimming fountains and empty cups;
  Beggars and nobles—peasants and kings:
These are a few of our downs and ups,—
  A part of the total of human things.

ANTICIPATION.

Anticipation is the oil that feeds
   The flame of life.   It is the Siren fair
That sings at twilight in the hollow reeds,
   And drowns the moaning discord of despair.
Nay, now in darkest night it comes to me,—
   It dulls the edge of every present care :
Blots from the tablets of the memory
   What hath been ill, or *is*, inscribing there
In golden letters that which yet may be
   Of earth's good things my individual share.
And should the days be drearier in age,
   And disappointment part of mine estate,
With fortune I shall not a warfare wage,
   But sing my song as now,—as now anticipate.

PAST AND FUTURE.

The Past!—In even our oldest songs
　　Regret for older past appears,—
The Past with all its bitter wrongs,
　　And bitter, buried years:
With all its woes and crimes and shames,—
　　Its rule of sword, and king, and cowl—
Its scourges, tortures, axes, flames,
　　And myriad murders foul!

The Future! To our latest lays
　　A common strain of longing clings
For future nights, and future days,
　　And future thoughts and things.

The Future! Who of us will see
   This Future,—in its brightness bask?
Ye ask the Future?—Let it be!
   Ye know not what ye ask.

'Tis best,—let Folly still lament
   The past, or for the future yearn,—
With this large *Present* well content,
   To watch, and work, and learn:
Assured that, if we do aright
   What must by us to-day be done,
The three shall open to our sight—
   Past, Present, Future—*One!*

See the poet's final recursion below

153

THE BEST PHILOSOPHY.

If there be aught of light behind
    The grave's sepulchral gloom ;
If this, so-called, immortal mind
    Shall triumph o'er the tomb,
Man well may laugh at death, and find
    A pleasure in his doom.

Or if Omnipotence decrees
    A harsher fate to men,
If Truth, and Love, and Joy, if these
    Shall not be ours again,
What is of good 'twere well to seize,
    And laugh in life even then.

Ay, this is best philosophy,—
    The present to enjoy ;
To trust but little what may be
    Our after-death employ,
Since after-life is mystery,
    And Hope—a fragile toy !

WITH A FAITH.

With a Faith
  So firm, so full, so reverent as thine,
Triumphant trampling over life and death—
  All but divine,—

Hold it fast!
  For earth hath many winning voices, each
Striving to win the people from the past
  With cunning speech!—

I could win,
  Methinks, some solace in this world of ours,
Transforming to rich music its rude din,
  Its weeds to flowers:

With a Faith.

Life's wild storms
  To calms : its darkness all to light,
And its most hideous and repelling forms
  To beauty bright.

I could live
  In proud defiance of Earth's utmost scorns ;
Pluck all the joys existence had to give,—
  Shun all the thorns.

I could die
  Calm as a foam bell on a placid wave,
Calm as a love-lit dream. yet living I
  Would be—a slave.

AT THE CROSS-ROADS.

To which hand shall I turn ?
That road upon the right ascends the hill,
Abrupt, all but impassable :
   This on the left, as I discern,
Winds down the vale beside the wimpling burn
And lake star-fair and still :—
   To which hand shall I turn ?

   Shall I not walk in this—
The left, the smooth and ever pleasant way;
Where birds shall greet me as I stray
   With strains oracular of bliss ;
Where every care I may dismiss—
Where all is garden-gay,
   Shall I not walk in this ?

   No—in the other. Why ?
The one road was so bitter, bleak, and bare,
The other was so wonderfully fair,
   With every gift to please the eye,—
With sun and shade and flowers and song,—
How should I choose nor choose the wrong ?
   One word I heard—" Beware ! "
So paused and pondered long.

ON LIFE'S SEA.

On Life's sea ! Full soon
  The evening cometh—cheerless, sad, and cold ;
Past is the golden splendor of the noon,
  The darkness comes apace—and I grow old.

Yet the ship of Fate
  Drives onward o'er the waters mountain high !
And now the day goes out the western gate
  And not a star is smiling in the sky.

Gloom before—behind !
  Rude billows battling with an iron shore
On either hand : anon, the chilling wind
  Smiting the cordage with an angry roar.

Then the compass veers
  And doth avail not : for the dust of earth
Hath marred its beauty, and the rust of years
  Hath made its mechanism of little worth.

On Life's Sea.

And tho' oft I gaze
  Into the lost, yet ever lovely Past,
And strive to call a power from perished days
  With which to dare the midnight and the blast,

The power flies my hand ;
  And my sad heart grows wearier day by day,
Beholding not the lights which line the land
  And throw their smile upon the desert way :

For the star of Hope
  Shed but one beam along the lonely path,
Then slid behind the clouds adown the slope,
  And set forever in a sea of wrath !

Yet the ship moves on—
  Aye, ever on ! still drifting with the tide,
With Faith alone to look or lean upon,
  As pilot o'er the waters wild and wide.

Yet for all, I feel
  My bark shall bound on billows gentler rolled,
Be Faith my pilot, then, until the keel
  Shall kiss and clasp the glittering sands of gold !

ALL HEART-SICK.

All heart-sick, and head-sick, and weary,
  Sore wounded, oft struck in the strife,
I ask is there end of this dreary,
  Dark pilgrimage, called by us Life ?

I ask is there end of it—any ?
  If any, when comes it anigh ?
I would die not the one death but many
  To know and be sure I should die.

To know that the sighing and sadness
  Should vanish and leave not a trace,
Although never a sunbeam of gladness
  Should shine on my soul in its place.

To know that there was no Hereafter—
  Hereafter of sorrow or joy ;
No time of mirth, music or laughter,—
  Not a moment of time of annoy.

To know that somewhere in the distance,
  When Nature shall take back my breath,
I shall add up the sum of existence
  And find that its total is—death !

New York 1879.

THE ROSES AND THORNS OF LIFE.

Ah, well! 'Tis as old as this world of ours,—
    The few are born to the couch of ease,
But the great men only—these, ah, these
    Are born to the thorns and not the flowers.

And He who made it so best knows
    What is our good; and so the man
Goes forth, fulfilling nature's plan,
    Grasping the thistle—passing the rose.

THE MAYFLOWER.

(IMPROMPTU)

You ask me, dear friends, a toast to propose ?
　Let me think for a moment—ah, yes ! it shall be
The sweet-scented blossom that blooms 'neath the snows,
　The sweet little Mayflower for me.

You may drink to the thistle, the shamrock, the rose,—
　May they each bloom on Liberty's shore ;
But my toast is the Mayflower that blooms 'neath the
　snows,
　The bonniest, best of the four !

'The National Emblem of Nova Scotia.

EDGAR ALLAN POE.

Though all the world forbear, Columbia weep :—
   Guard well the grave where Edgar's ashes sleep ;
Let fairest flowers and rarest lilies grow
   Where sleeps in dust thy noblest genius—Poe !

QUID REFERT?

"They had lived and loved, and walked and worked
in their own way, and the world went by them. Between them and it a great gulf was fixed: *it* cared nothing for them, and *they met its every catastrophe with
the Quid Refert? of the philosophers.*"

*DE LA ROQUE.

What care we for the winter weather,—
    What care we for set of sun,—
We, who have wrought and thought together,
    And know our work well done?

What do we care though glad stars glitter
    For others only? Though mist and rain
Be over our heads? Though life be bitter,
    And peace be pledged to pain?

Quid Refert ?

What care we ?   Is the world worth minding,—
  The sad, mad world with its hate and sin ?
Is the key worth seeking for, or finding,
  Of the Cretan maze we wander in ?

What care we though all be a riddle,—
  Both sea and shore, both earth and skies ?
Let others read it !   We walk that middle,
  Unquestioning way where safety lies.

And care not any for winter weather,
  And care no more for set of sun,—
We who have wrought and thought together,
  And know our work well done !

Myself, G. F. C.

WHEN EVERY HOPE.

When every hope the heart hath held
And every joy the heart hath known
  Depart, yet leave a soul unquelled
In moody grandeur on its throne,
  I sigh—and wish it all my own :—
I sigh, and wish such spirit mine
  That I may soar above distress
And prove that man may be divine
  In his own native lordliness.

  But what my fate ?—To weave in song
My idle fancies, and to grope
  With troubled spirit through the throng
From fear to fear—from hope to hope:
  And if I sometimes strive to cope
With these forebodings of the soul,
  Too soon, alas ! I feel and know
'Tis but a Samson-hand can roll
  The stone upon the tomb of woe.

ON ———

A singer, I admit : but hath his song
   E'er eased the sad, sick soul, e'er dried the eye
Of secret sorrow, bruised the head of wrong,
   Or woke the heart to listen to the cry
Of Right down-trodden by the despot-throng ?
   No ?   Then, so please you, we will put him by.
   He is a poet ?   Never !   I deny
He hath a portion of the sacred rage.
All flowers of speech may bloom upon his page,—
   His soft words on my senses idly fall :
Not having any utterance for his age,
   He hath no power to stir my blood at all ;
So off with him to moulder on the shelf !—
He knows not man, nor any God save self.

ON McDONALD CLARKE.

(THE MAD POET)

Unhappy, penniless, alone!
  With doubt before, and debt behind;
With reason tottering on her throne,
  And love a bitterness, being blind:

With passions much too largely framed
  For his poor body to control,
He went his way all unashamed
  And wooed the muse with all his soul.

So, poets, take him from the throng
  Of weaklings who have feigned to wake
The lyre, and name him in your song,
  And crown him for the muse's sake!

TO——

Not often, in these latter days
  Of gloss and glass and overpress,
Do poets by the world's highways
  Pluck plumes of everlastingness.

Not often—where the eagle sweeps—
  About the sun-swathed crags of ice,
Do they, uprising from the deeps,
  Reach forth and pluck their edelweiss.

Not often.—For the elders took
  The best of fancy's flowers so fair ;
Or, passing, in their frenzy shook
  All trees and left the branches bare.

And yet, methinks that thou hast found
  A something—subtle as a sense ;
A something—sweeter than a sound,
  Which means eternal eminence.

A FACE.

I mark at a window over the way
   A woman who sits most patiently there
Whose face is as pale as a stellar ray—
   As pale, and as pure, and as fair;—
A face you might look upon all the day,—
   A face like a beautiful petrified prayer!

JOHN MILTON.

A name not casting shadow any ways,
   But gilt and girt about with light divine;
A name for men to dream of in dark days,
   And take for sun when no sun seems to shine—
Thou sightless wearer of immortal bays,
   Thou Milton of the sleepless soul is thine!

THREE SONNETS.

ON LEAVING NOVA SCOTIA, 1874.

I.

Farewell! And I must speak the word to-day;
  And I must leave what I have known so long,—
  And only known to love, and loved to know!
The breeze moves strongly outward from the bay,—
  And here and there amid the busy throng
Affection wrings the hands of those who go,
  And love as deep the hearts of those who stay.
The feast is o'er, and sad the parting song!
Why not? These hills our feet have trod in youth:
  Why not? These vales our earliest vision knew:
Why not? These friends—we long have prov'n their
    truth:
  And now to each and all we bid adieu!
The lines are cast: loud rings the warning bell:
Swift clasp of hands, brief kiss,—and long farewell!

Three Sonnets.

II.

I stand alone at midnight on the deck,
    And watch with eager eye the sinking shore
Which I may view, it may be, nevermore :
For there is tempest, battle, fire, and wreck,
    And ocean hath her share of each of these,—
    Attest it, thousand rotting argosies,
Wealth-laden, sunken in the southern seas!
    And who can say that evermore these feet
Shall tread thy soil, Acadia?   Who can say
    That evermore this heart of mine shall greet
The loved to whom it sighs adieu to-day ?
Our sail is set for countries far away;
    Our sail is set, and now is no retreat,
Though Ocean should but lure, like Beauty, to betray !

III.

When shall I see them all again ? I say,
  Now that the loved, lost land lies far a-lea,—
Now that we are upon the world's highway,
  Now that we are alone upon the sea.
When shall I meet them all, when shall it be ?
  When shall I come to them, if ever ?　When
Shall I come back to these dear ones again ?
Speak, ocean-winds ! Is it beyond your ken ?
  When shall I come to them, or they to me ?
I hear no tone ; no token gives the wind :
  The only voice is where above the shrouds
The sea-mew screams defiance to the clouds :
  Till Night comes down, about, before, behind,
And locks all lands from sight, but locks not mine from
    mind !

TRUE GREATNESS.

What is true greatness?   Is't to climb
  Above the rocks and shoals of time
To sculpture on some height sublime
      A name
To live immortal in its prime
  And flush of fame?

What is true greatness?   Is't to lead
  Your armed hirelings on to bleed,
And move a terrible god, indeed,
      An hour;
To sate your lust of gold, or greed
  Of despot power?

True Greatness.

What is true greatness?   Question not,
   But go to yon secluded spot
And enter yonder humble cot
      And find
A husbandman who never fought
   Or wronged his kind :

For whom the lips of war are dumb :
   Who loves far more than beat of drum
The cattle's low, the insect's hum
      In air :
And find true greatness in its sum
   And total there !

What is true greatness ?   'Tis to clear
   From sorrow's eye the glistening tear :
To comfort there, to cherish here,
      To bless :
To aid, encourage, and to cheer
   Distress.

TO JOHN RHODE.

A POSTAL.

From Tybee, John! from joyless Georgian Tybee,—
    From godless, graceless Tybee by the sea,
Whereon at present a sojourner I be,
    A word from me!

Fill high the bowl—and fill it to o'erflowing!
    High let the flagon flash, and flare, and foam:
For Thursday next I'm going, going, going,
    I'm going home.

I hate to leave—God bless the loves!—the ladies
    With their dark eyes and smiles that thrill me so;
But, *peste!* the atmosphere is hot as Hades,
    And I must go.

So please the gods, then, and the wind blows steady
    And favoring, Monday next I'll blow the foam
From off a cup,—be sure and have it ready!—
    With you at home!

Tybee Island, Georgia, June, 1882.

TYBEE.

Lone Ultima Thule, fare thee well !
   Upon thy ocean-battered shore
   If it should be that nevermore
In all this life my eyes should dwell ;

If it should be that 'neath thy shades,
   No more in rapture to my breast,
   When the red sun is in the west,
These arms shall clasp thine amorous maids ;

If it should be, that I shall gaze,
   When the broad moonbeams on it sleep,
   No more upon thine emerald deep,
I bow to Fate's mysterious ways :

And, leaving in the hands of Him
   Who threads the future through and through
   The few who stay, the faithful few,
Say only, as the woods grow dim,

And as the wild-voiced sea winds swell,—
   Say only, as I wave my hand
   For the last time out toward thy strand,
Lone Ultima Thule—fare thee well !

Atlantic Ocean, off Tybee, June, 1882.

INSULÆ FORTUNATÆ

Oh, for a breeze from the balmy islands,
　The fortunate islands and blest of the sea !
Vine-lands or pine-lands, lowlands or highlands,
　So they be summer lands—nought care we.

Here are we thralled by the autocrat hoary
　And heartless—the hater of lily and rose—
Winter, who gives us no gleam of the glory
　And brightness and bloom that the summer-time
　　knows.

Here Love lies dormant or dead for a season ;
　Joy plumes her wing for less desolate clime ;
Hope flings farewell to us, giving no reason ;
　Faith even goes star-ward to tarry a time.

Insulæ Fortunatæ.

Pæan Apollo, disdaining to linger,
  Calls to his lovers of song and of shine,
Calls those who love him, and, pointing the finger
  Fair to the southward, goes over the Line.

So then, of sweetness, of summer forsaken,
  What is the wonder that ones who are wise
Sigh for the isles where forever men waken
  To scent-laden airs and to song-laden skies?

What wonder we long for a breeze from the islands—
  The beautiful islands and blest of the sea?—
Vine-lands or pine-lands, lowlands or highlands,
  So they be *summer* lands—nought care we!

Kingston, November, 1882.

TO MY BROTHER CHARLEY.

Though others fail or fly,
   Thou wilt not fail me—thou !
I read it in thy clear, calm eye
   And steadfast brow.

Whate'er of good or ill
   May chance with time or tide,
To me and mine unchangeable
   I feel thou wilt abide.

Though my high hopes decay,
   Though summer-friends depart,
I know that thou wilt cling alway
   To me, heart of my heart !

Until Life's storm subsides,
   And o'er the billow's crest
My vessel all victorious rides,
   Or lies a wreck—at rest.

THE GOLDEN TEXT.

You ask for fame or power?
  Then up, and take for text:—
This is my hour,
  And not the next, nor next!

Oh, wander not in ways
  Of ease or indolence!
Swift come the days,
  And swift the days go hence.

Strike! while the hand is strong:
  Strike! while you can and may:
Strength goes ere long,—
  Even yours will pass away.

Sweet seem the fields, and green,
  In which you fain would lie:
Sweet seems the scene
  That glads the idle eye:

The Golden Text.

Soft seems the path you tread,
  And balmy soft the air,—
Heaven overhead
  And all the earth seems fair :

But, would your heart aspire
  To noble things,—to claim
Bard's, statesman's fire—
  Some measure of their fame ;

Or, would you seek and find
  Their secret of success
With mortal kind ?
  Then, up from idleness !

Up—up ! all fame, all power
  Lies in this golden text :—
This is my hour—
  And not the next, nor next !

Boston, 1882.

'THE "WEEK" vs. WENDELL PHILLIPS.

I.

They sneer at *him* who ever wrought —
   Disdaining any earthier aim, —
To keep whatever God begot
   As something—something worthy name!
   A man whose breath was fan and flame
To blight and blast a bitter wrong:
   Who held it as his fairest fame
To cheer the weak and curb the strong?

II.

They sneer at *him* who was a foe
   To every man that menaced man!
Who went, as brave hearts always go,
   To cannon lip and battle van; —
   Who never owned a rout, nor ran; —
Who, till the final field was won,
   Up from the day the fight began
Still bared his breast to wind and sun!

<hr />

In answer to a virulent attack upon the dead orator which appeared in the columns of the Week directly after the announcement of his death.

III.

They sneer at *him* who dropped and died,—
　The harness on him—in the way;
Who ever taught and ever tried
　To date a good from every day;
　Who spoke when Freedom went astray
And waked and warned and won her, too,
　With words that die not, nor decay;—
Still *to be Freedom*, and be true!

IV.

They raise their voice and rail at *him*
　Who was as high above their ken
As stars that in the zenith swim
　Are high above the heads of men!
　Back to forgetfulness again
When they and theirs alike are fled,
　This Phillips' work of lip and pen
Shall ride on earth high-charioted!

MAN, BOAST NOT OF THY FRIENDS.

Man, boast not of thy friends, until
  They have been tried in fortune's flame:
Until, in day of pain and ill
They friendship's holy vows fulfil,
And prove that time can change nor kill
  What is forevermore the same.

Wait, till thy faltering footsteps tread
That dim, mysterious, distant, dread,
  To us unknown abode;
If then thou hast but one true friend
  Who trod with thee life's journey o'er,
Weep not to part!—such steps will tend
Together yet; such souls will blend
  Like music—on another shore.

DISCONTENT.

The morning's mirth, the midnight's grief,
 These wait on each and all of us —
On yonder slave, on yonder chief—
 The great one and the small of us.

We fain would fly the future *fact*,—
 Avoid the very way of it;
But every deed we do, each act
 Of ours but draws the day of it.

We fret like foreigners on earth
 And fools, and cry:— O shame of it !
Why had we being, why had we birth,
 To bend and bear the blame of it ?

Why did we ever see the sun,
 When we must see the set of it ?
'Twere well if day had ne'er begun,
 For all the good we get of it !

1883.

TO WENDELL PHILLIPS.

A FRAGMENT.

O eloquent-lipt last lover of mankind,
　　Full-veined apostle, blest of God above!—
Hath Death the dark, the bitter and the blind—
　　Called halt, and clipped thy mission work of love?

Far in the dim and undivined somewhere—
　　In what hope holds as better yet-to-be,
Drinking deep draughts of more immortal air,
　　We hope to meet, and walk, and talk with thee.

February 3rd, 1884.

MY FAITH.

I would not blot the star of Hope
    That hangs so palely in the skies :
But, giving thought a larger scope,
    And following wheresoe'er it flies,

I find I hate nor sects nor creeds,
    Yet have a creed all creeds above,
Whose faith consists in noble deeds,
    Whose highest law is highest love.

And thus I do not feign, but feel
    A different faith from thee, my friend !
And yet, perhaps, through woe and weal
    They both lead on to one grand end.

I AM YOUNG.

I am young, and men
    Who long ago have passed their prime
Would fain have what I have again,—
    Youth, and it may be—time.

To gain these, and make
    Life's end what it may not be now,
Monarchs of thought and song would shake
    The laurels from their brow.

And each king of earth,
    Whose life we deem a holiday,
For this would give his kingship's worth
    Most joyously away!

THE POET'S REASON.

You ask me why I write, yet print not? I
   Have heard there lived far back in the past ages
A mighty sage amid the mighty sages
   Of earth, and one whose name may never die,
   Who thus was questioned, and did thus reply:

I cannot practise that I preach, and so
   I must not preach the thing I cannot do:
But it is meet for self to take a view
   Of inner and of outward things, although
These thoughts or things be neither nice nor new.

And when these musings into verse will flow,
   I hold it right to keep them to myself,
   Nor lumber up my neighbor's groaning shelf!

TO THE WEST WIND.

West wind, come from the west land
    Fair and far !
Come from the fields of the best land
    Upon our star !

Come, and go to my sister
    Over the sea :
Tell her how much I have missed her,
    Tell her for me !

Odors of lilies and roses—
    Set them astir ;
Cull them from gardens and closes,—
    Give them to her !

Say I have loved her, and love her :
    Say that I prize
Few on the earth here above her,
    Few in the skies !

Bring her, if worth the bringing,
    A brother's kiss :
Should she ask for a song of his singing,
    Give her this !

Boston.

TO LOUISE.*

My Sister ! It is long since thou and I
　　Have been together, and it may be long
Ere we shall meet again : thou dwellest nigh
　　Our childhood's home : I mingle with the throng,
　　Though thou dost know I do not there belong ;
For I abhor the spirit of the mart
　　That makes our air an atmosphere of wrong ;
That checks the growth of every noble art,
And poisons each pure spring that issues from the heart.

Earth hath not much to love : but soon I learned
　　To love those things it hath of good or great ;
To noble deeds and noble words I turned,
　　And marked my own bright pathway.　If stern fate
　　Hath changed its proper current, mine estate
Is not less noble : I shall walk alone,—
　　Not with a mien defiant and elate,
But in humility,—and if I own
No kinship with the crowd, to them 'twill not be known.

Mrs. Stewart, New Glasgow, Nova Scotia.

To Louise.

But Fate is lord, and we are slaves of Fate:
  His wish, his will, his word our law supreme;
And we, perforce must touch the things we hate,
  Though such was not our own fantastic dream:
  For we are only bubbles on a stream,
And as the torrent goes, we too must go,—
  Now wrapped in darkness, now by Cynthia's beam
Made beautiful and bright: and if we know
Nought of our final end, 'tis best it should be so.

Yea, this is as it should be: for if we
  Could only know in youth what we must know
When youth is ours no longer, few would see
  The summer sun of life; for most would go
To probe at once the spell of mystery,
  And sound its dreadful depth of weal or woe:—
Would free the bird, and spurn the narrow cage,
Nor wait to taste the marah of old age.

Which would be most unwise. It is so sweet
  To drink life's chalice to its very lees;
To crush the daisies with your dotard feet,
  And mourn departed opportunities;

To Louise.

To see your hopes wrapped in their winding-sheet ;
   To spend your days and nights upon your knees ;
To live a dreary life, a weary slave,—
To tumble trembling to a dismal grave.

But let us dream awhile that we are free,—
   Free as God's azure ! Casting care aside,
Be once again the things we used to be,
   Ere I had drifted out upon the tide,—
   Ere I had sailed on seas unsanctified ;
Ere thou had'st put the mantle of the maid
   Away, to wear the mantle of the bride :
Stray once again where once our footsteps strayed,
Play once again beside the stream where once we played.

Come, let us dream our bosoms still contain
   The essences of pleasure ; that the bloom
Of happy youth is on our cheeks again !
   Come, let us drive away each thought of gloom
   That in our breasts hath ever yet found room !
Come let us roam together hand in hand,
   And pluck the flowers full-freighted with perfume—
With dew-drops sparkling, and by south-winds fanned,—
The flowers that gem the fields of our beloved land !

To Louise.

Come, while the world grows old, we will grow young!—
    Read o'er again the books we wont to read,—
Methinks I hear the accents of thy tongue
    As thou dost say, " We may do this, indeed,
    But all the rest—?" I pr'ythee still take heed!—
Or, let us watch the reapers as they reap,
    Or watch the boats that down the river speed:
To-day on pleasure pleasure let us heap,—
To-morrow we shall wake,—perchance, to-morrow weep!

To-morrow waken? I have wakened now!
    The scene grows dim, and broken is the spell:
The lines of age come back upon my brow—
    The heart grows older than the tongue can tell:
    Enchantment, Beauty, Pleasure—all farewell!
Oh, blame me not, Louise, that I did call
    Illusion to delight me from her cell!
Her tone was sweet as ever yet did fall
On mortal ear:—alas, 'tis silent soon and all!

Each sunny-featured fancy fades away;
    Stern, iron-visaged Duty claims her due:

To Louise.

Melts as a dream the prospect garden-gay,
　　Which but this moment recollection drew,—
　　And forth I fare to face the fray anew.
Well, there are honors in all wars to gain,—
　　And be my chaplet laurel-leaves or yew,
And be the sequel pleasure all or pain,
This much will Time attest,— no fight is fought in vain !

Whatever moves, the end is recompense
　　For every action, whatsoe'er the end !
In this I have 'gainst every ill defence,
　　How thick and fast soever ills impend :
　　And if at times the body chance may bend,
O'erburdened pilgrim ! weary in the way,
　　I deem the stronger spirit still will lend
　　A faith and strength unto the weaker clay,
That it may well endure—until the close of day !

SIC TRANSIT.

A noble record! so he said in pride,
　A noble record, and right nobly won,
　Which ages yet to be shall look upon;
A noble record! so he said—and died.
And, lo! the years came up from out the sea
　Of time; like dreams all old things passed away—
　The bud that gave rich promise yesterday
Of fair and fragrant immortality
　Dropped faded, withered—ceased for aye to be,
And with it died the poet's proudest lay.

WHAT THEY MEANT.

(IMPROMPTU)

There is a man—an Ishmaelite,
  Who never (hardly) does a square thing,
Got drunk, alas! one Sunday night,
  Which was—alas! again—no rare thing.
Whose friends all prophesied that he
  (Of course they said it not in malice!)
Would break his neck upon a tree,
Or have it broken, so you see
'Twas just the same to you, and me,
  And him,—they meant the gallows.

THE WAY OF THE WORLD.

We sneer and we laugh with the lip—the most of us do
  it,
   Whenever a brother goes down like a weed with the
     tide ;
We point with the finger and say—Oh, we knew it! we
   knew it !
   But, see ! we are better than he was, and we will abide.

He walked in the way of his will—the way of desire,
   In the Appian way of his will without ever a bend ;
He walked in it long, but it led him at last to the mire.—
   But we who are stronger will stand and endure to the
     end.

His thoughts were all visions —all fabulous visions of
   flowers,
   Of bird and of song and of soul which is only a song ;
His eyes looked all at the stars in the firmament, ours
   Were fixed on the earth at our feet, so we stand and
     are strong.

He hated the sight and the sound and the sob of the
city ;
He sought for his peace in the wood and the musical
wave ;
He fell, and we pity him never, and why should we
pity—
Yea, why should we mourn for him—we who still
stand, who are brave?

Thus speak we and think not, we censure unheeding,
unknowing,—
Unkindly and blindly we utter the words of the brain;
We see not the goal of our brother, we see but his going,
And sneer at his fall if he fall, and laugh at his pain.

Ah, me ! the sight of the sod on the coffin lid,
And the sound, and the sob, and the sigh of it as it
falls !
Ah, me ! the beautiful face forever hid
By four wild walls !

You hold it a matter for self-gratulation and praise
To have thrust to the dust, to have trod on a heart
that was true,—
To have ruined it there in the beauty and bloom of its
days ?
Very well ! There is somewhere a Nemesis waiting
for you.

O LADY FAIR AND DEBONAIR!

O lady fair and debonair,
  Why dost thou weep in darkness there!
Why mourning now? why dost thou bow
Thy flower-like head and starry brow
  Crowned with so wondrous wealth of hair?
Those eyes of thine were made to shine—
So deep their hue is and divine—
Where love and light and beauty bright
  Do make a splendor of the night.

Now, pardon me, but, can it be
  That love has proven false to thee?
Speak, lady, speak! Hath Love been weak
And sought afar a fairer cheek?
  Then Love must seek it over sea.
Nay, should he roam afar from home
For fairer o'er the farthest foam,
His task is done—his race is run :—
  There is no fairer, lady, none.

O Lady Fair and Debonair.

Forgive me still, since sin I will—
  Though not to work thee any ill—
But, hath there been of sons of men
One loved who did not love again,—
  Whose breast hath proven invincible?
Then, lady, know—'tis better so:
Forgive, forget, and let him go!
Since he hath shown his heart was stone,
  Lo, I will sacrifice mine own.

Thy pardon, yet!—I did forget
  The weightier ills that do beset:
Did lightly speak, and vainly seek
The reason of thy pallid cheek,
  Bowed head and heart, and eyelids wet:
Some bitter woe, some fearful blow
Hath touched thee thus, it must be so:
So at thy feet I bend me, Sweet,
  And beg thou wilt thy tale repeat.

O Lady Fair and Debonair.

Ah ! Arctic Death with sudden breath
　Hath touched thy bud—Elizabeth ?
Then, let her lie, nor vainly sigh ;
We, all of us—were born to die :
　But look to Him of Nazareth !
As marble cold, of marble mould
Is she whom thou dost vainly fold
Now to thy breast : but, being blest,
　I pr'ythee, lady, let her rest !

BUNKER HILL, *1885.*

A RONDEL.

Ten years ago a boy reclined
  Where Warren won his fatal blow,
And sung what passed within his mind
  Ten years ago:

  While idly in the soft June wind,
The palm and pine rocked to and fro,
  And spake to eyes that were not blind

Of a defeated South, resigned
  To meet in peace her old time foe,
And of a conquering North, but kind,
  Ten years ago.

I wrote some verses on the occasion above referred to—June 17th, 1875,—the one hundredth anniversary of the Battle of Bunker Hill. The Palmetto and the Pine were planted side by side on the hill.—G. F, C. June 17th, 1885.

HOPES AND FEARS.

A RONDEL.

With hopes and fears the gods still try us
   Each and all through the winding years:
The past is past, and the morrows defy us
   With hopes and fears.

   Naught that is stable and sure appears:
We reach for power—'tis sure to fly us,—
   And the oftener still as the churchyard nears.

We reach for rest, while the world wheels by us
   And leaves us each in our vale of tears,
Till the green sod covers and naught comes nigh us
   With hopes and fears.

June 17th, 1885.

OH, NEVER MAY THE SHADOW OF THE PAST.

To———

Oh, never may the shadow of the Past
   Upon thy path fall grimly : never may
Thy summer sun be shrouded and o'ercast :
   May peace be ever with thee on thy way !
And if a thought shall come to thee at last
   Of him who loved thee in his better day,
Kind be that thought, and void of all regret,
For he who loved, if living, loves thee yet.

AS SOME SWIFT STAR.

To———

As some swift star that through the azure slips,
    Led by a secret, passionate desire,
Forever moving in her bright ellipse
    With eager pinion towards the central fire
Thy course hath been! and through the upcoming years
    I hold no doubt that it will be the same,——
    Unto the morning-light of noble fame.
And this it is that most to me endears
    Thy song; for thou dost cherish still the pure,
The true—the wise. In every noble line
I see the beauty of thy large design,
    And feel, sweet singer, thy reward is sure:
So, all delighted, watch each flight of thine,
    And wait to see the praise thou wilt secure!

"OUR BOYS."*

We thought them and called them and held them "Our
    boys"—they are men :
    They have stood at the lip of the cannon and felt its
        hot breath :
They have heard of the hiss of the ball, and again and
    again
    They have looked in the face of death.

We sent them away to the battle with many a sigh,
    With many a tremor of heart. and with many a tear;
And, now that the day is their own, let each shadow go
    by,—
    And welcome them home with a cheer !

---

* Who served in the North-West rebellion—1885.

14

"Our Boys."

With the flaunting of flags, and the ringing of bells, and
    the sound
  Of the trumpet and cannon, whose voice they have
     heard in the fight.
Let us show we are proud of our boys who all ready
    were found
  To battle like men for the right.

So welcome them back to their mothers, and sweethearts,
    and wives ;
  And remember forever and ever, whatever befal,
That in perilous moments they gallantly perilled their
    lives,—
  And honor them each one and all !

ERE THE MOON THAT WANES.

Ere the moon that wanes to-night again shall largen,
  Ere the sun that sets to-night shall set again,
You and I may be beyond the bound and margin
   Of the death and doubt that makes the death a pain.
    For, albeit Time's wheels move slow,
      Time's wheels move steadily still ;
    And when they go, we go,
      And when they pause, we will.

You may reap a golden harvest—I may reap less ;
  I may wear a motley mantle, you a crown :
But I feel unto the valiant and the sleepless
  Meet reward the powers above us will cast down.
    To Him who watched by day,
      And watches all night through,
    Will come a perfect pay—
      Rich reckoning and true.

Ere the Moon that Wanes.

He who knew what weariness and want and woe meant,
  He who pillowed Earth's sad head upon His breast,—
He who bore that one unutterable moment
    When the burden of her sorrow on Him pressed : —
      To Him, we deem, was given,
        For answer to His love,
      All things on earth—in heaven,
        All love below—above.

Fear no loss !　Although the shadows close and thicken,
  Just beyond the shadow surely lies the light :
If it be not so, we are, at best, but stricken
    Back, who were brought forth of Night, again to night.
      Fear nothing—nought is lost !
        Life, freedom, love, and truth
      From sphere to sphere are tost :—
        Here have they but their youth !

THEY SAY I SING TOO SAD A STRAIN.

They say I sing too sad a strain,
    And question of the reason why :
    I know not,—but it seems that I
Sang gaily once : I may again
    If that which makes me sad goes by.
There is a mystery of joy
    In each and every woodbird's trill ;
The song of man, the song of boy
    Have more of loss and ill.

The song of man, the song of boy
    Have more of pain : though, it may be,
'Twas but some trifling, slight annoy,
    It leaves a sadness in his strain—
A darkness in his every song ;
Just as the cloud in yon inane—
    An aery nothing seemingly—
Leaves, as it floats above, a long
    Dark line of shadow on the sea.

TO JOHN CARRUTHERS, ESQ., GLENVALE.

Oh, I have heard of welcomes, yes !
   Of highland ones and others ;
But none of them surpass, I guess,
In pure and simple heartiness,
   A welcome by *Carruthers*.

LORD BYRON.

On hearing it averred that the works of Byron were
too immoral to be read, and that, for that reason, all
memory of the poet should quickly perish.

I think your judgment incorrect:
    For he, though sometimes not too moral,
Like Cæsar hides his sole* defect
    With an immortal laurel.

---

* Cæsar's sole defect was a crown defect—he was bald; so he covered
his head with laurels. —G. F. C.

WITH ALL MY SINGING.

With all my singing, I can never sing
  A gay, glad song —an honest song of mirth :
In vain my fingers seek some tender string
  Whose voice would catch the dainty ear of earth.
Why is it so ?   Because the fount and spring
  Of all my song was sorrow ; it had birth
In gloom, and desolation, and dark hours,—
'Twas not the offspring of the happy flowers.

TO CHARLEY.

Hast thou the poet-gift ?   Thou hast,
  O golden-tongued and hearted Greek !
  To find thy prototype, I seek
Far down along the shadowy Past,
  Where half-gods and whole poets speak :

Wit, song, and eloquence divine—
  Where are they in the list of names ?
  I halt at his of many fames,
And boldly call thee, brother mine,
  A Sheridan—without his shames !

TO MY DAUGHTER JESSIE.

On her first birthday.

My little gem !—a dearer gem
    Than ever flashed since Adam's fall,
Or so to *me* than all of them, —
    Yea, more to each than all.

Save one, my mother's, 'neath the sky
    No lovelier lip hath ever smiled ;
Nor ever beamed a kindlier eye
    Than that of thine, my child !

Kingston, July 8th, 1885.

THE DAYS OF LONG AGO.

A SONG.

Bring back, O Time! bring back to me
  The days I once did know,
The dear old days that used to be—
  The days of long ago!

Bring back the hopes that failed to last.
  The fears that failed not so :
Bring back, bring back the golden past—
  The days of long ago!

Bring back the loves I won and lost
  Through Love's inconstant flow ;
Bring back, bring back, at any cost,
  The days of long ago!

The Days of Long Ago.

Bring back once more the fruit and flower,
   The early morning glow,
And give me for a single hour
   The days of long ago.

O Autocrat divine and strong !—
   For men have called thee so,—
Bring back with summer and with song,
   The days of long ago.

Vain, vain ! I know it—my request ;
   They come not once they go
However bright, however blest—
   The days of long ago.

BECAUSE !

"O woman, in our hours of ease,"
   As Scott has somewhere said or sung,
So very difficult to please,
   So sweet of lip, so swift of tongue,
   I've often tried, since I was young
And danced you darlings on my knees,
   To find out why you have not kept
From Time's rapacious, greedy jaws
   A reason for your whims, except
That old moth-eaten one—"Because !"

Why is it ?   Hath there never been
   A time in all the tides of Time
When female tongue or female pen
   In rhymed prose or prosed rhyme
   Hath given an utterance more sublime
And pleasant to the ears of men ?
In all the ages that have slipped
   Since that old ark of Noah's was,
Hath never dear young woman lipped
   A better reason than—"Because !" ?

Because !

Not one!   The summers come and go,
   The ages dwindle to a span,
And woman sweet can only throw
   These self-same syllables at man.
   Yea, from Beersheba unto Dan,—
While men, the brutes! have reasons plus
   For finding faults, or forging flaws,—
The Fates have shackled woman thus
   To mild, monotonous—"Because!"

And as it was and is, it will
   Be ever till the years grow pale
And die with very age ; until
   There is nor female left nor male ;
   Until the sun himself shall fail :
For this is woman's last resort,
   Parenthesis, and saving clause,
And period still in sense or sport,
   Her exclamation point—"Because !"

Kingston, '83.

THE LAND OF DREAMS.

There is a land where rolls along
  A thousand gilded streams,
The half enchanted son of song
  Names it the land of dreams.

Sweet warblers hang on every bow,
  And softened twilight gleams
Eternal o'er the mountain's brow
  In this dear land of dreams.

With amber drops the luscious vine
  Bows to the foliaged ground,
And myriad warblers from the pine
  Send harmony around.

The Land of Dreams.

With argent tint its limpid lakes
  Embrace the silver streams:
Reality alone awakes
  Ye from that land of dreams!

And wandering through the lofty halls
  In upper realms of air,
Where not a footstep's echo falls
  To break the stillness there,

I met a being fair as day,
  Her eyes like night, I ween,—
A sweet, fair angel gone astray,—
  My own, loved, lost Ellene.

Ysolte.

Our love and our hate! This life of ours,—
  Whatever life's law above,—
Is woven of thorns of hate, and flowers
  And sharpest thorns of love:

And all of our webs of romance or truth
  Take their color and tone from these;
And as it is now in the world's wild youth
  It shall be through the centuries.

Ysolte.

Well, I am young and the world is wide,
  And I have gold enough and to spare,
And I could buy, if I would, a bride
  To give me, perchance, a son and heir :
But single my heart is, and I will abide
As single, and float on my own gulf-tide
  Of desire, now here, now there,
Wherever my silver shallop may ride
  And my sails of silver bear,—
Until I drift on the unknown shore,
And beach my boat to roam no more.

How easily men are caught with chaff !
An ankle, an eye, or a light-lipt laugh,
  And down they go on their knees.
Was I caught myself ?   Oh, not by half !
  No, thank you, if you please.
I will be caught ?   No, thank you, again !
  I sound myself on all these things,
And find I am not like the most of men
  To be led in leading strings.
No painted, or pretty, or perilous girl
  Shall put my soul in pain :

Ysolte.

No ruby lips o'er teeth of pearl,
Gazelle-like eye, or wind-kist curl
　　Shall break my heart in twain.

Oh, I do laugh to see men cringe
　　Before some delicate, dainty doll,—
Some mass of foolishness, fuss, and fringe,
　　Some delicate—nothing at all.
To see men fawn and flatter and lie—
　　At the feet of these dolls, I mean,—and swear
That they for sake of them would die,
　　They might die did they dare :
For men in love are fools—or nigh,
　　Though cap nor bells they wear.
To see them, knowing so well man's mind,
　　And knowing so well that woman's power
　　Is that of beauty, but of an hour ;
And knowing well of womankind,—
　　To see them and hear—oh, I do laugh !
　　Why are they crows to be caught with chaff.

Oh, I do weep to see men creep
   Through mire, and dirt, and deadly shame,
To drag the gold from its æon-sleep
   Or to snatch a kiss from Fame.
Can place or power avail to keep
   Star-clear a tarnished name ?
Well, what of this ? But this, no more :
   For dunces we need not rake the schools ;
For the most of men—'twas said before—
   Are arrant fools—are arrant fools.

And now that my say is said of men.
   I leave them alone, and nothing loth :
Let them sink to themselves, if they will, again,—
   To their love and life—I leave them to both.
For I am young and the world is wide,
   And I have gold enough and to spare,
And I could buy, if I would, a bride
   To give me, perchance, a son and heir ;
But single my heart is, and I will abide
As single, and float on my own gulf-tide
   Of desire, now here, now there,—

Ysolte.

Wherever my shallop of silver may ride
   And my sails of silver bear,—
Until I drift on the unknown shore
And beach my bark to launch no more !

Here shall I end my days !
   No longer Ishmael-like I roam.
Here, where the natural streamlet plays,
   Here, where the innocuous cattle graze,
Where other foot but seldom strays
   Than mine, I find a home.
Yea, on this eminent mountain's breast
   Where calm winds meet :
The sun-kist river seeming blest.
Wrapt in perpetual peace and rest,
   Low-lying at my feet,
Dividing me from man and mart
   And wrong and turmoil consequent
And all of ill, at length my heart
   Is well content, is well content.

Ysolte.

Companionship ? Enough for me
    My books and birds and flowers ! if bliss
    In any place more perfect is,
In any place can any be
    More innocent than this ?

I have no fear of present wrong ;
    I cannot dream of future ill,—
        Against the demon of regret
        My pride must prove an amulet :—
    With these as dear companions still,—
The wood-bird with his happy song,
    The columbine and daffodil.
    And these book friends unchangeable
Beside me all day long.

No, I may sleep and wake each morn
    To say—To-day no city strife
Shall shake my peace, or press a thorn
    Into the flesh of life !

Ysolte.

It seems as if a change
  Had come across the earth,—
A something sweet and strange:
  Gone is the gloom and gone the dearth
  Of sunshine and soft air and mirth,—
I feel as if again a boy;
  Departed is my old annoy.
And all is life and peace and joy
  Befitting second birth.
I have been born again;
  And in my new-found mood
I say that beasts and birds and men,
  All things that are or that have been,
Are good—are very good.

But will it, can it last—
  This life that is so sweet?—
Where all the past is past
  And buried 'neath my feet?
Can it be as a shadow cast—
  Not real, but a cheat?

I think not.   It is said,
   When one is born anew
That all the former life is fled
   And that then present true.

Is't substance, or a sham ?
   I know the stars shine brighter
      Than they before had shone :
The air is warm and calm :
   I know my heart is lighter,—
      Its heaviness is gone:
I do not lean on broken reed,—
This is a newer life indeed.

And so, since I am sure
   This new world is secure,
I, who have never tried to sing
   Since in that old world I was young,
Since that first youth was in its spring,
Will strike again a merry string
   And sing as I have sung :—

Light, light, light !
  The morning is breaking at last :
The darkness is dead, and the night—
  The desolate night is past.

Joy, joy, joy !
  The shadow that haunted me so,—
That clouded the life of the boy
  And the life of the man, may go.

Earth, earth, earth
  Swings round to a heart-prompted tune ;
The day is delivered of mirth,—
  December is genial as June.

Love, love, love
  Hath broken the ancient spell :
There is beauty below and about and above,
  And the soul that was sick is well.

Fear, fear, fear
  Of a future that never may be ?
No ! the future is *there*, the present is *here*,
  And that is enough for me !

Ysolte.

There is a stranger in the place,
   A stranger who no doubt looks down,
Scorn on his lip and ashy face,
   Upon the God-made country clown.
   And he is stopping there in town :
And he has seen the one I love :
   And he will love her—that I know,
   A voice within me tells me so.
But, sooth, I swear by the stars above,
   By the tides at my feet that ebb and flow,
   Whatever may come, whatever may go,
He shall not harm my harmless dove.

I swear he shall not harm her ! still,
Her lord shall be her own sweet will.
And if her own sweet will shall put
   My love aside, I shall but say—
This trampling true love 'neath her foot
   For false, is only woman's way.

His face is lined and worn, although
   'Tis fashioned fairly and might pass—
A female mirror flatters so—
   At muster in a lady's glass :

234

Ysolte.

But his hand is as a lady's fair,
  His foot is as his hand is—small ;
  So should you take them all in all
They would be quite a pretty pair.

The prowling fox has found his prey,—
  An easy prey, an easy prize :
So easy that some people say
  It was a willing sacrifice.
But I say neither yea nor nay,
  Not having other people's eyes.

He angled and she took the bait.
  Perchance he used a noble line
And golden hook,—at any rate
  He has no reason to repine :
If I have reason, ' Such is fate !'
  I say, or—' Such is fate of mine !'

Love is the serf of Mammon : we,
  Being serfs of love, are doubly slaves.
Were it not better, then, to flee

Ysolte.

From both and to our graves —
Those sanctuaries where neither can
  Force homage from the knee of man?

The heart is most deceitful — truly so!
  Late when I dreamed I dreamed not I did dream:
  And things that seemed to seem not did but seem:
And what I knew I knew I did not know.
  'Twas in a vision that upon the stream
  I cast my lotos-leaf, and it did glide
  Adown it till I thought 'twould stem the tide:
But far beyond my sight it gathered weight,
And sank at last — o'erburdened with my fate!

I am on earth once more!
  My hope, by one foul breath,
Is driven upon an iron shore, —
The mad, wild waters whelm it o'er
  And deed it unto death.
I am most bitterly alone!
  The stars are distant, dim and cold:
  This is the old life o'er — the old!
Where is the new that I have known?

Ysolte.

They are together much of late,
　They passed me by to-day:
I was standing there at my gate :
　He nodded a cloudy brow—not ill,
She shot me a smile as they rode away
　To the house beyond the hill :
I would hate him could I hate,—
　If I learn to hate, I will.

And yet, why hate him ?   He
　Who falls by woman's wile
Should only have pity from me :
　I will pity him—after awhile,
When she from her heart and love
　Hath cast him aside and out
Like a toy she is wearied of,
Or flung him away like a glove
　Torn or soiled at a rout.

I will afar, and leave behind
This love as fickle as the wind,—
　Will seek a newer solitude ;

At once away, for to my mind
  There is no good, there is no good
In anything of womankind.
I will away from haunts of men
  To live the old life o'er and o'er,
  To live the life I lived before,
To be,--but I will say no more,--
  To be again—what I have been!

Be what I have been? No!
  The gates of the Past are closed;
  And no one, even if so disposed,
Behind those gates can go:—
Those gates—precipitous and steep—
  They never rest ajar;
And only memory can sweep
  Over them, whil'st their guardians are
Bound in the cords of sleep,
  And dreaming softly in their star.

What! Go to what I have been? to
  The darkness and the gloom
  Of the cold, voiceless, soulless tomb,

Where love-light moves not through,
From all that I of late did know
  To that old life—I cannot go!

He who hath sometime scanned
  The stars that gem the sky,
The sea and lovely land,—
  All beauties that delight the eye,
All things that He hath planned
  Or here below or there on high,
And then hath lost his sight,
  Hath fuller cup of bitterness
  To quaff than he would ever guess
Whose eye hath never seen the light.

And I,—I who have sometime stepped
  Upon the paths of Paradise,
Where odorous opening roses crept
  Up palms whose tops were in the skies,
Where waves of melody were swept
  Full tide from throats of birds who kept
  No reckoning of their song, nor slept,
But made the day and happy night
  In perfect circles of delight,—

Isolte.

How can I ever find again
   A pleasure in the desert wide
   Where all the springs of life are dried.
Where all the nightingales are men
   Who ever sing in songs of woe?
How can I close my ears and eyes?
   To that old world how can I go,
Nor sigh for sights and melodies
   That there I may not know?

It would not happen as it did,
   It would not have been but for him!
Did not my better self forbid,
It may be there is something hid
   Which I could tell him that would dim—
But, no!—'tis little to my mind
   To undermine her woman-whim;
Besides, I will not be unkind.

I will forgive, perchance forget;
   To time and tide leave all the rest;
She may find life is bitter yet,
   Ay,—find it bitter on his breast

Without a sign from me, or threat ;
  For life is bitter—at the best !

Oh, that we had not met to part
  As we are parted now,—
The stain of anger on each heart,
  Of anger on each brow !

Would that the love which shone so bright
  Had killed me with its blaze ;
Ere I had seen it robed in night,
  And robb'd of all its rays !

Would that the hours so fleet and fair
  Had never come to me !—
Ere I had known that once they were,
  That they no more can be.

Would I had slept the dreamless sleep,
  Ere I had come to know
That Love may sow in joy, yet reap
  A harvest wild with woe !

Ysolte.

Would love had faded ere my birth
   Or blossomed on my tomb :
Nor ever mocked my youth with mirth,
   To curse my age with gloom !

And oh, that we had never met
   And dreamed a dream of bliss,
To wake again to cold regret,
   To wake again to—this !

*   *   *   *

Where often I have found relief,
   I went to seek for peace to-day,—
A temporal balm for temporal grief :
     Amid fair Nature's solitudes,
     Within the ivy-fretted woods.
I found it in a novel way.

Upon the moss beside a spring
Whose limpid waves go spattering
   Adown the ancient rocks and gray,
   As often I had lain I lay

Ysolte.

When to my hand came wandering—
  The wind had tost it there in play—
A vagrant scroll bound by a ring,
  A golden circlet old and thin.
I seized it, and half jestingly
  Spake to it, opening, " Let me see
What omen may be here for me!"
  And this is what I read therein :—

"WHAT THOUGH, MY BROTHER"—

What though, my brother, to-day be drear
  And dark and sad ?
To-morrow, to-morrow will soon be here—
  Perchance to make thee glad.

Sorrow and heaviness—these are things
  That come to men :
They come to the commons, they come to kings,
  They come to go again.

Why should a season of bitterness bear
  Thee down to dust ?
To-day may be foul yet to-morrow be fair ;
  Trust in to-morrow—trust !

243 [over]

Ysolte.

And if to-morrow be darker yet
  With pain and ill,
Though the heart be dry and the eyelids wet,
  Trust in to-morrow still!

It was enough,—a hopeful song!
  Had some good genius sent it here,
Borne on the kindly winds along
  Inscribed with promise of good cheer
  For some dear future day or year?
I may be right, or may be wrong;
  But thus I will interpret what
  The day and accident have brought:
Perhaps there is a generous Fate,
  A generous Fate! but time will tell
  If all be ill or all be well,—
And, for the present—I can wait.

Though she be false as coquette's kiss,
  From this sweet mood I must not stir
  In which Love, as interpreter,
Reads all the auguries for bliss;
But bring myself to chime with this,—
  'Tis well, if all be well with her.

Ysolte.

Yes, yes! O Love—lost Love of mine!
    If thou wert with me now to-day
And peace and happiness were thine.
    Though sad my soul I still would say:—

If thou art happy, all is well!
    I care not what remains to me;
Though nought but ill my stars foretell,
    'Tis well, so all is well with thee!

Affection's flower may fade and fall;
    Life's fairest promises may flee:
I hold it recompense for all
    To know that all is well with thee.

The star of faith may quit my sky,
    The compass fail me on Life's sea:
My bark may wreck, but what reck I
    'Tis well, so all is well with thee!

Though hope and all I hold be vain,
    'Twill shorten still, where'er I be,
My hour of bitterness and pain
    To know that all is well with thee!

Ysolte.

As out of elemental motion life
  Comes forth to man and health and strength,
  Out of the war of words at length,
Out of the stir and storm and strife
  Comes forth a sterling hope to me—
  A hope of better days to be.

Into the field comes gallant Truth,
  In mail arrayed and armed with flame,
  To champion a tottering fame
That else were martyred in its youth.

Now, clear the lists ! an even start !
  Spur, Slander—Truth ! They meet nor part.
Now, Sword, be true as God is just !
  As God is great be great, O Heart !
Ah ! Slander smitten smites the dust :
  The knight of Truth is o'er his head :—
  The liar and the lie are dead !

Now hear the end of all the play !—
  I hold her fair and firm and true
  To eyesight and to soul-sight, too :

She is the sweetest piece of clay
   God ever sculptured into form !
And who on earth shall say me nay,
   If to the wide, wild world I say,
Until life's storms forever stay,
   I shall defend her from all storm !

I hear along the air a wedding bell ;
Say, heart of mine ! how is it ?
              It is well !

Lyrics on Death.

Draw the dread curtain and enter in !—
    In o'er the threshold the millions have trod :
Lose but the dust of the balance, and win—
    What a moment ago was the secret of God !

September, 1885.

AN ANSWER.

"Can it be good to die?" you question, friend;
    "Can it be good to die, and move along
Still circling round and round, unknowing end,
    Still circling round and round amid the throng
Of golden orbs attended by their moons—
    To catch the intonation of their song
As on they flash, and scatter nights, and noons.
    To worlds like ours, where things like us belong?"

To *me* 'tis idle saying, "He is dead."
    Or, "Now he sleepeth and shall wake no more:
The little flickering, fluttering life is fled,
    Forever fled, and all that *was* is o'er."
I have a faith—that life and death are *one*,
    That each depends upon the self-same thread,
And that the seen and unseen rivers run
    To one calm sea, from one clear fountain head.

I have a faith—that man's most potent mind
    May cross the willow-shaded stream nor sink ;
I have a faith—when he has left behind
    His earthly vesture on the river's brink,
When all his little fears are torn away,
    His soul may beat a pathway through the tide,
And, disencumbered of its coward-clay,
    Emerge immortal on the sunnier side.

So, say :—It must be good to die, my friend !
    It must be good and more than good, I deem ;
'Tis all the replication I may send—
    For deeper swimming seek a deeper stream.
It must be good or reason is a cheat,
    It must be good or life is all a lie.
It must be good and more than living sweet,
    It must be good—*or man would never die.*

Boston, April, 1878.

REST.*

Of that deep sorrow that befel
   Even yet I cannot calmly speak,—
When we who knew and loved him well,
   And saw the roses on his cheek
            Fade week by week,

Stood by his bed, and knew that One,
   Unseen, beside us held a place,
And waited but for set of sun
   To lay cold hand upon his face
            And steal its grace :

In memoriam of Charles Pritchett.—Died June 10th, 1871.

Rest.

And knew that One but waited near
  To seal the eloquent, loving lips ;
To rob the spirit of its dear
  Earth robe,—from heart to finger-tips
              To make eclipse.

And knew the all that we had need
  To know—that God had need of him :
And some there seemed to see, indeed,
  The sweet fair forms of seraphim
              Winged, moving dim

About the couch whereon he lay
  Who yesterday was in the bloom
Of youth and strength,—but yesterday !—
  And round about the darkened room,
              And through the gloom.

Rest.

I scarce can calmly speak, though years
   Have touched me since, of him and all
The alternating hopes and fears
   That swayed us, till the golden ball
            Of day did fall :

And Death and Night, his sister, met
   And came together to the bed ;
Ah ! Love was vain as amulet
   To drive the harpies from his head,
            Or they had fled.

They came—twin Night and Death—they came,
   And on his veins their fingers prest,
And calmed the blood that was as flame,
   And stilled the beating of his breast.
            And gave him rest !

SHELLEY.

I.

"Dust unto dust?" No, spirit unto spirit
   For thee, beloved! for thou wert all fire,
   All luminous flame, all passionate desire,
All things that mighty beings do inherit,
   All things that mighty beings do require.
"Dust unto dust?" Ah, no! Thou did'st respire
   In such a high and holy atmosphere,
   Where clouds are not, but calms, and all things clear,—
Not one like ours, but purer far and higher,—
Thou did'st not know of dust. How "dust to dust"
     then here?

Shelley.

II.

Spirit to spirit, be it! Thou wert born
  An heir apparent to the throne of mind.
  It lessens not thy right that some were blind,
And looked on thee and fixt a lip of scorn,
  And threw on thee the venom of their kind :
Thou wert a brother to the sun and wind,
  And it is meet that thou art of them now.
  I see thee standing, with thy godlike brow
High-arched and star-lit, upwardly inclined,
While at thy feet the singers of sweet song do bow.

III.

For spirits are not as men : *these* did not know
  An angel had been with them on the earth,—
  A singer who had caused a glorious birth
Of glorious after-singers here below,—
  Where much was sung and little sung of worth.
I see the stars about thee as a girth,—
  The moon in splendor standing by thy side,
  And lesser moons that evermore do glide
About her circling, making songs of mirth,—
And o'er thy head supreme Apollo in his pride,—

IV.

Pleased with the homage that his children give thee,
  Remembering it as *his*, even as thou art ;
  Knowing thy heart a portion of his heart,
And spreading forth his breast as to receive thee-
  Twin soul of his, that had been rent apart.
I leave to marts the language of the mart.
  Ashes to ashes say above the crust
  Of him who *was* but ashes,—it is just !
But over *thee* as homeward thou did'st start,
Spirit to spirit was true, and not "dust unto dust !"

March 21st, 1883.

DEAD!

Dead!   And the north wind whistles o'er the place
    Where they have left her in her youth and bloom,
The snow of winter heaped above her face,
So fairly spread it scarcely leaves a trace
    Even of her tomb!

Dead!   And she leaned to life with such a love
    That death seemed more than hateful to her eye ;
For though she never found a doubt to move
Or shake her faith in better things above,
    'Twas hard to die!

UNTIMELY.[*]

Untimely! So we say, and sigh,
  Is any hour so then for rest!
Is any hour so then to die,
  When dying is being blest?

Not one! And though our dead may reach
  No hand to us, nor come and tell,
We have *within* a voice whose speech
  For death is ever--all is well!

This voice within, and all without
  Confirming it, affirming still
That past this ill, and death, and doubt,
  There is nor doubt, nor death, nor ill.

So wish her not from her repose,
　And ask her not!—though that were vain
As 'twere to ask a full blown rose
　To close and be a bud again.

And mourn not! She, where nothing mars
　The perfect rest, the perfect good,
Beyond the circle of the stars,
　Escaping nether womanhood,

With all the evils that attend,—
　Uncertain fortune, much annoy,
Attains at once the endless end—
　The peace, the palm, the calm, the joy.

Ay, there! beyond the burning track
　Of morn, where angel pinions stir,
She waits for us,—she comes not back, ―
　She waits for us,—*we go to her!*

*ON THE DEATH OF A CHILD.

Dear boy! yea, dear as if thy years
   Were many, thou art gone to rest
And with the happy in the spheres
   Allotted to the blest.

We miss thee sadly, yet, perchance,
   'Tis well that thus our dream should lose
Its glory-mantle of romance,'
   And all its gorgeous hues.

For, though our cup, being broken. holds
   No more for us hope's holy wine,
We know that the Omnific folds
   Thee to his heart divine.

Alfred, infant son of Lt. Col. McLelland Moore, and nephew of the author
C. J. C.

On the Death of a Child.

We read fair fortune for thee, read
  Enough of days and nights of joy,
With tropic suns and moons which shed
  A lustre o'er thee, boy !

We built for thee our castles fair,
  Proud, golden-turreted, sublime,
By streams which ran through pastures rare
  In our green island—Time.

But whil'st we read, and built, and plann'd,
  An angel came and wooed thee hence
And won thee from our lower land
  To God's high eminence !

IN MEMORIAM.

"LIEUT.-COL. MACLELLAND MOORE,* one of the
first commissioned officers appointed by Governor And-
rew for active service in the Rebellion.

＊　　　＊　　　　　　　　　　　　　　　　　＊

His name was a familiar one in old time military circles, with which his connection began thirty years ago
(1852) as captain of the American Artillery, at the age
of sixteen. At the outbreak of the Rebellion he went
into service for the Union as Captain of Co. E in the
"Old Eleventh"; subsequently he was promoted and
transferred to the Twenty-Eighth Massachusetts as its
Lieutenant Colonel.

Of the value of his services the war records furnish
due testimony, and broken health and long years of
suffering bear evidences of his sacrifices. Possessing
besides his sterling military qualities, an instinctive
taste for science and literature, he blended with the
love of duty the graces of a genial spirit."—*Boston
Journal*.

---

*The author's brother-in-law.—C. J. C.

In Memoriam.

I.

O brother ! dust and ashes ! dust
 Upon the tongue so sweet in song,
Upon the lips so true, and just,
 And cunning to denounce the wrong :—
 And ashes in the hands so strong,
And swift to war it for the right ;—
 And ashes on the heart so long
A thing of love, and life, and light !

II.

And can it be that he is dead
 Beside that river that I know ?
And is there heaped upon his head
 The burthen of the New Time's snow ?
 And shall the seasons come and go,
And mellow moons still wax and wane,
 And birds still sing, and blossoms blow,
And we desire his voice in vain ?

In Memoriam.

III.

And must we mingle with the crowd,
    While close the nights, and come the days,
And dream of one no more allowed
    To walk beside us in our ways;
    Or only look with upward gaze,
And hope beyond the mystic end
    To meet once more, without amaze,
The husband, brother, father, friend?

IV.

Yea, dreams of what did once befall,
    However dim the dreams, or old,
And hopes of what may be—are all
    These mortal hands of ours may hold.
    We have no more; the tale is told;
The wondrous web of life is spun;
    I look aloft—the stars are cold,
    But in the East I see the sun!

In Memoriam.

V.

And from the utmost heights I hear—
    Sheer down the waste of waveless sea,—
A voice that whispers in my ear
    That all that still is mist to me
    Is clear as noon to him, that he
May now, where cloud nor darkness mars,
    With eye that longed to see them—see
The solemn secrets of the stars !

VI.

So, let him sleep ! The stir, the strife,
    The toil, the turmoil all are o'er ;
He will not wake, nor leap to life,
    At sabre-clash, or cannon roar ;
    He takes the battlefield no more,
Nor wakes at any dawn of day,
    But, with his comrades passed before.
Waits the diviner Reveille !

January 24th, 1884.

DEATH.*

Dear friend, I know this world is kin,
    And all of hate is but a breath :
We all are friends, made perfect in
    Our near relationship by death.

And so, although it was not mine
    To meet thee in thy walk below,
Or know of thee till feet of thine
    Were on the hills no man can know ;

For friendship's sake I fain would bring
    A flower, or two, to thee to prove
That memory lives, that death's sharp sting
    Hath still an antidote in love.

Death.

Devoured by his desire of her
   The king, who ever loved her best,
   Hath stilled the billowing of her breast,
Hath kissed her so no pulse doth stir,
   But all of her doth lie at rest.

Then, knowing she may never now
   Wish any else, he takes his leave,
   And little recks how they may grieve
Who see the splendor of her brow
   Gleam ghastly through the gathering eve;

Who see her lying pale, supine,
   With wild red roses twined with fair
   About her throat, and in her hair,
And on her bosom,—all divine
   If but a little life were there.

Nor heeds he aught the sunless glooms
   And fair forms folded from the light
   In close graves crowded far from sight
In lone lands dedicate to tombs
   And scarce to starbeams known at night;

But goes his way; and as he goes
   Leaves that we hold as sorrow here, —
   The pain of parting and the tear,
The broken lily and the rose
   Down fallen with the fallen year.

Cold king, most lone and absolute!
   What maid would be desired of thee?
   From thy embrace who would not flee?
What though a monarch, being mute
   In love of thine what love could be?

Can any good be silent so?
   Be dumb, and do its work and pass
   Swift as an image in a glass?
Ah, all of good that we can know
   Thus comes to us, and leaves, alas!

While we, who have no key to ope
   Death's cabinet of mysteries,
   Can only vainly strain our eyes,
And hold to heaven and that high hope
   That death is good in any guise!

     *   *   *   *   *

And if but slight to thee appear
   The tribute brought, now that thine eyes
May view through all the eternal year
   The fairer flowers of Paradise,—

If dim and all unworthy look
   The offering, yet remember well
We do not sleep by Eden's brook,
   Or dream on beds of Asphodel :

So only bring the flowers that bloom
   Beside us, fresh enough and fair ;
Enough to wither on thy tomb :
   And with our hearts—behold them there !

A YEAR AFTER.

A SONNET.

Who of us thought upon that gay May night,--
   That night of joy, and jollity, and cheer,—
   That two, within the circle of a year,
Two of our number should have passed from sight—
   Passed from this present to another sphere,—
Passed through death's darkness out into life's light?
Not one of us now living. Happy all,
   We wished not morn, nor sighed for yesterday:
We gave no thought to funeral pomp or pall,
   Or gnawing worm, or darkness, or decay.
Yet are they gone: and we, who yet remain,
   Grasp but this lesson: it is ever thus,—
Though pleasure drown awhile all thought of pain,
Though we forget of death, yet Death forgets not us.

Boston.

IN MEMORIAM.*

I.

On many a heart a shadow falls,
  Where lay a line of light of yore,
For here, within the College walls,
  And there, beyond the College door,
    A friend—that time shall not restore,—
Is missing—leaving not a trace—
  Is missing, and forever more
Is missing from his wonted place !

II.

And as the sad word onward slips
  From hall to hall, from room to room,
The laughter freezes on our lips,
  And lo !—we speak of death and doom
    And grief comes in to us and gloom,—
With swift suggestions of a soul
  That waves at length a perfect plume.
Or waits—a winner—at the goal !

*John C. Macleod, Captain of Queen's College Football Team.

In Memoriam.

III.

And though he only seemed to dwell
   An instant with us, ere the Foe
Laid hand upon him and he fell,
   Down-smitten by a bitter blow,—
    We knew him ; we were glad to know :
And these shall miss him in the class,
   And those shall miss him as they go
To meet their rivals on the grass.

IV.

And long his memory shall remain,
   And be amongst us and abide—
Though he shall not return again
   With any time, or any tide ;
    For dark Death's river is, and wide ;
And long our eyes shall seek our friend
   Who wanders on the other side,—
Where we shall find him in the end !

Queen's College, February 16th, 1884.

FROM THE SEA.

A FRAGMENT.

A voice comes in with the tide,—
    A voice that I should know:
And I fancy it that of the dead, who died
    Ah, me ! so long ago.

With the solemn sigh of the sea
    The voice comes landward in :
And ever it seems to say to me—
    Death wins not—Life doth win !

Sacred.

What care I for faith of fathers or of brothers?
   All this written faith is nothing: there is faith.
Yea, as high as God is high above all others
   Over every precept—over each Thus Saith.

Oh, there are various arts and many
   Held holy by the throng,
But unto me the round world holds not any
   More so than that of song.

   *   *   *

Let us praise the great God with our hearts not our lips,
   With deeds that shall speak, not with simper or sigh:
Devotion of soul needs no saddening eclipse,—
   Let us please and be pleased for to-morrow we die!

LORD GOD ALMIGHTY.

Lord God Almighty ! Thou who art
   The sire of all the orbs that roll,—
The head of each, the hand, the heart,
   The centre and the soul !

My Refuge, Rock and dear Desire,
   While ills on ills about me throng,
Shall I not come to Thee, the Fire
   And Fount of all my song ?

And as thou did'st from wrath of Saul
   Deliver David, forced to flee,
So, when in pain to thee *I* call,
   I know thou'lt succor me.

Lord God Almighty.

For thou art not a God afar,
　But ever present, ever nigh,
And ready still in every star
　To hear thy children's cry.

Oh, I have sinned and I have strayed
　From Thee, the Shepherd of the flock,
Have scorned Thy guidance, and have made
　Thy law divine a mock:

Again and yet again have done
　The wrong, and wandered from the right;
Have followed folly with the sun
　From early morn till night.

But, like the prodigal, my heart—
　Too long undone and desolate—
Seeks Thine, believing that Thou art
　As good as Thou art great!

1883.

HE IS RISEN !

"He is risen! He is risen!" Hear the universal chorus;
  Note the number of the nations—hear them now, they
    all rejoice;
Lifting to the stars above us, to the sweet stars swim-
    ming o'er us
  One united thankful voice
        That He is risen !

He is risen—the Redeemer ! Earth nor Death nor Hell
    could bind Him,
  For His strength was all immortal like His own im-
    mortal love :
Vainly to the place of burial go the maidens out to find
    Him :
  Ah ! the angels far above
        Know He is risen !

He is Risen.

He is risen! In his rising ends the world's divinest
  story,—
  One that still shall find an echo while earth eddies
   round the sun ;
One of sadness wov'n with gladness, one of gloom and
  one of glory.
  One that tells us, All is done! Earth is won!
    And—He is risen !

He is risen ! He is risen ! Lo, the gentle Gallilean
  Whom they crucified and buried leaves the tomb and
   takes the throne :
Leaves the cross, and, while the peoples fling the palm
  and raise the pæan,
  Reascends and takes His own,—
    For He is risen !

Easter Morn, 1885.

279

His Last Lyrics.

My spring is over, all my summer past :
    The autumn closes,—winter now appears :
And I, a helpless leaf before its blast,
    Am whirled along amid the eternal years
To realize my hopes—or end my fears.

September, 1885.

BEYOND THE UTMOST DOUBTS AND DEEPS.

Beyond the utmost doubts and deeps
  Where Chaos with her sister sleeps,
Beyond the crimson and the blue
  Which eye of man hath seen not through.
Beyond the spaces sounded not,
  There is, I feel, one nameless spot
Divine as Northern night in June
  With balmy breeze and mellow moon,
Divine as youth's dear dream of love,
  Divine as any star above,
As lovely as the day's first beam,
  As holy as the poet's dream,
As virgin as the garden trod
  By him who walked and talked with God.

And once it seemed to me I found
   Me in that consecrated ground,—
Yea, there I moved a visitor.
   And there it was I looked on Her.
I loved yet dreaded her. She knew
   Me calmly, kindly through and through.
She knew my virtues—I had few ;
   She knew as well my vices, too.
She read me as an open book
   And praised or punished with a look.
And sought and reached me wheresoe'er
   My spirit took me foul or fair,—
Aye, found me, as the river will.
   Or spring it from the vale or hill,
The blue, the broad, the boundless sea
   Where all its aspirations be.

For this I dreaded her, but then
   I never spake of dread to men :
But if they questioned me of her
   I called her still my comforter—
A something more than maid or wife,
   A love that only died with life :—

Beyond the Utmost Doubts and Deeps.

And life knows not of death: away
   Beyond the morn of earth and day,
Beyond its ground, beyond its gyves,
   Life all eternal still survives.
The snow may cover all the land:
   The rose may wither in your hand:
The lily shiver when shall fall
   About and o'er it Winter's pall:
But mark me,—whosoe'er may care,—
   The life that still is life is there!

September, 1885.

TO GOD. THE AUDITOR OF ALL ACCOUNTS.

To God the Auditor of all accounts
    We shall give up account of all our ill ;
And though in men's minds to a mountain it amounts
    Who knows but with His imitateless skill
            As recompense
    Adding and footing up sin's bill
He will find pounds of Good where man writes pence.
    And when I see Him I hope and pray
            Lifting the hands
            That framed all lands
    He will say—Benedicite !

September, 1885.

WHAT MATTERS IT?

I.

What reck we of the creeds of men ?—
  We see them—we shall see again.
What reck we of the tempest's shock ?
What reck we where our anchor lock ?
  On golden marl or mould—
In salt-sea flower or riven rock—
  What matter—so it hold ?

II.

What matters it the spot we fill
  On Earth's green sod when all is said ?—
When feet and hands and heart are still
  And all our pulses quieted ?
When hate or love can kill nor thrill,—
  When we are done with life and dead ?

What Matters It?

III.

So we be haunted night nor day
  By any sin that we have sinned.
What matter where we dream away
  The ages ?—In the isles of Ind.
In Tybee, Cuba, or Cathay,
  Or in some world of winter wind ?

IV.

It may be I would wish to sleep
  Beneath the wan, white stars of June,
And hear the southern breezes creep
  Between me and the mellow moon :
But so I do not wake to weep
  At any night or any noon.

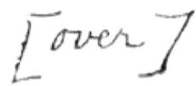

[over]

What Matters It?

V.

And so the generous gods allow
   Repose and peace from evil dreams.
It matters little where or how
   My couch be spread :—by moving streams,
Or on some eminent mountain's brow
   Kist by the morn's or sunset's beams.

VI.

For we shall rest : the brain that planned,
   That thought or wrought or well or ill,
At gaze like Joshua's moon shall stand,
   Not working any work or will,
While eye and lip and heart and hand
   Shall all be still—shall all be still !

HIS LAST POEM—MY FATE.*

Away and beyond that point of pines,
　　Away in a spot where the glad grapes be,
Purple and pendant on verdant vines,
　　That Fate of mine is awaiting me.

And if no more the wind blows true
　　To waft me afar to that island sweet,
Beyond that greater and other blue
　　I feel that I and my fate shall meet.

For the hope that is can never fade,
　　And the hope that is can never fall,
That Fate was law since the world was made,
　　That it shall be law till the end of all.

And Time may be long or it may be brief
　　Ere I stand on that dim and unknown shore,
And grief or joy be mine, but grief
　　Can dwell not there—where we meet once more.

---

* Found in his pocket after his death.—C. J. C.

L'Envoi.

To the Poets of the Past and Future.

THE PAST.

With reverent hands your books we close,
   O poets of the imperfect Past!
The East grows ruddy as the rose
   And tells us that the Night at last
Goes from our planet, banished with her woes:

Goes banished forth with all her wrong:
   While all her pontiffs, priests, and kings,
Who trampled on the weak, being strong,
   Are laid aside—forgotten things,—
And we must open up new books of song.

We give you justice.   In the days
   When Freedom knew not her own name,
Ye dared to know and sing her praise
   In words that fanned to fuller flame
Our own less rude, imperishable lays.

THE FUTURE.

O poet of the future!   I,
    Of the dead Present, bid thee hail!
Come forth and speak,—our speech shall die:
    Come forth and sing,—our song shall fail:
Our speech, our song fall barren,—we go by!

Our heart is weak.   In vain it swells
    And beats to bursting at the wrong:
There never sets a sun but tells
    Of weak ones trampled down by strong,
Of Truth and Justice both immured in cells.

We would aspire, but round us lies
    A maze of high desires and aims;
Would seek a prize, but, ah! our eyes
    Fail as we face the fallen fames
Of the great world's Olympian games.

The Future.

Seeing the victors vanquished, we
 Grow heartsick at the sight, and choose
To hold in fee what things there be
 Rather than in the hazard use,—
Than stake the all we have—to lose !

We all are feeble. Still we tread
 An ever-upward sloping way ;
Deep chasms and dark are round us spread
 And bale-fires beckon us astray :
But thou shalt stand upon the mountain head.

But thou wilt look with gladdened eyes
 And see the mist of error flee,
And see the happy suns arise
 Of happier days that are to be,—
On greener, gladder earth, and clearer skies.

We, of the Morning, but behold
 The dawn afar : thine eye shall see
The full and perfect day unfold,—
 The full and perfect day to be,
When Justice shall return as lovely as of old.

The Future.

Thou, with unloosened tongue, shalt speak
   In words of subtle, silver sound,—
In words not futile now, nor weak,
   To all the nations listening round
Until they seek the light,—nor vainly seek !

We only ask it as our share,
   That, when your day-star rises clear,—
A perfect splendor in the air,—
   A glory ever, far and near,—
Ye write such words—*as these of those who were !*

Kingston, September, 1885.